The publication of this catalogue

is made possible

through the generosity of

The Best Answer in Banking

THE DIXON GALLERY AND GARDENS

The Home of Hugo and Margaret Dixon, c. 1950.

Photograph by André Kertész, 1952.

THE DIXON GALLERY AND GARDENS

ERIC A. CATMUR

WITH CONTRIBUTIONS BY

RICHARD R. BRETTELL

JOSEPH S. CZESTOCHOWSKI

GEORGE PLUMPTRE

MEMPHIS, TENNESSEE

Combined text and illustrations copyright ©1996 by The Dixon Gallery and Gardens.
All rights reserved under International and Pan-American Copyright Conventions.
Published in the United States by The Dixon Gallery and Gardens.

Library of Congress Catalog Card Number: 96-086845
ISBN: 0-945064-01-2

First Edition

Photographs on pages 6, 19, 24, 26,161 by André Kertész, 1952.

Catalogue research prepared by Marie Busco.

FOR

MARGARET OATES DIXON

HUGO NORBERT DIXON

Contents

Acknowledgments

The Dixon Gallery and Gardens is honored to present this publication celebrating the legacy of Margaret and Hugo Dixon. Through their 1976 bequest to the Memphis community, the lives of countless individuals have been enriched. At the young age of twenty, The Dixon Gallery and Gardens is a fully formed institution of regional, national, and international importance. For that we are indebted to the Dixons and the many friends and supporters who have nurtured their dream.

The involvement of Eric A. Catmur and S. Herbert Rhea, past Chairs of the Dixon Board of Trustees, was instrumental in creating the dynamic organization that is the Dixon today. In merely two decades, these leaders have achieved a productive balance of growth and stability that eludes so many not-for-profit organizations.

Joseph Orgill, III, as the third Chair in the Dixon's history, embarks on our third decade of growth. A perceptive leader, teacher, and mentor, Mr. Orgill's sense of humor and perspective never fails to calm and inspire. His leadership in finalizing the acquisition of the Ritchie Collection was invaluable, as was the support of numerous other individuals – those on The Dixon Gallery and Gardens Board of Trustees, The Hugo Dixon Foundation, the Life Members Society, Young at Art, and the Memphis Garden Club. All have significantly contributed to what we today affectionately refer to as "the Dixon."

Thank you to all who have contributed to this publication. Eric A. Catmur's detailed introduction reveals his close friendship with Margaret and Hugo Dixon and his invaluable knowledge of the museum's founding. Long time friend of the Dixon, Dr. Richard R. Brettell has provided an insightful essay about Hugo Dixon and Montie Ritchie. Dr. Brettell's interest in the Dixon promises continued growth in the content and quality of the collection. George Plumptre, editor of *Sotheby's Preview* magazine, has written extensively on traditional English country homes. His scholarly essay presents an intriguing interpretation of Hugo Dixon as the creator of such a home in Memphis.

We thank the following individuals for their assistance in this publication: Dr. Marie Busco, Alex Apsis, Cyanne Chutkow, and Francois Daulte. The catalogue design and production are by Elvis Kee of the Memphis College of Art and Edward Garavelli of Pinnacle Press. On the Dixon staff, my special thanks to Carissa Hussong for effeciently managing the completion of this project. Her enthusiasm changed a difficult time table into a beautiful publication. Staff members Sally Kee, Jane Faquin, and Deborah Bass also devoted time and energy on the project.

Above all, we acknowledge our benefactors, whose generosity and foresight created The Dixon Gallery and Gardens. May Hugo and Margaret look down on this twentieth celebration with the knowledge that their dream is a work-in-progress. The Dixon, at twenty, is on the brink of adulthood. There will be no stopping the progress that has defined it since its birth.

Joseph S. Czestochowski
Director

The Dixon Legacy

JOSEPH S. CZESTOCHOWSKI

The Dixon Gallery and Gardens opened to the public on January 25, 1976, fulfilling the wishes of its founders only two years after their deaths. Margaret and Hugo Dixon would have relished the inaugural exhibition, which highlighted the works they had so lovingly collected, including their last acquisition, Mary Cassatt's *The Visitor*. On this twentieth anniversary of The Dixon Gallery and Gardens, we celebrate the generosity of its founders with the presentation of this publication.

The Dixon is often referred to as the "jewel" of the Mid-South. Indeed, its development as a purely private entity with many-faceted programs reaching out to the public dazzles the mind in a world where most museums are centuries old. Actually, the history of The Dixon Gallery and Gardens began some time before the idea of creating a public space occurred to Mr. and Mrs. Dixon, and is linked by two separate events – the Dixons' decision in the late 1930s to build a home in Memphis with the esteemed Houston architect, John Staub, and the Dixons' first art purchase in the 1940s.

Like many collectors, the Dixons' continuity of vision began with a single purchase. For each of us – "collectors" or not – there is a defining moment in the first acquisition. The Dixons' moment struck in 1944 when they chose William James's *View of Venice*, a selection which reflected Mr. Dixon's English heritage. While this work did not define the ultimate direction of their collection, it ignited a passion for art that would develop over the next thirty years. Their passion was of the best sort, enabling them to enjoy their art in harmony with the home and gardens they created. They foresaw the inextricable relationship among the architecture of their home, the fine arts with which they chose to adorn it, and the surrounding seventeen acres of carefully planned gardens.

The Dixons never considered themselves professional collectors. As Hugo and Margaret agreed, collecting was an "investment in pleasure," and their tastes evolved naturally over time, from the English painters of the Grand Manner, to Barbizon painting, and eventually to the French Impressionists for which the collection is known today. Once their passion for Impressionist art had been established, the Dixons sought the advice of their close acquaintance, John Rewald, noted scholar of Impressionist art. He later reproduced one of their early purchases, Camille Pissarro's *Springtime in Eragny*, in his landmark book *The History of Impressionism*, published in 1973. This work was later donated to the Memphis Brooks Museum of Art during Hugo and Margaret's lifetimes.

The decision to leave their entire estate to the Memphis community is as much a part of the Dixon as are the collections and gardens. In his essay, Eric A. Catmur, the first Chairman and one of the founders of the Dixon, describes his personal relationship with Margaret and Hugo, and the events which led to the formation of The Dixon Gallery and Gardens. The Dixons and the other founders of The Dixon Gallery and Gardens – D. Nelson Adams, Lawson F. Apperson, Evelyn J. Boyle, Eric A. Catmur and Norfleet R. Turner – shared a unified vision of an art museum of the first rank. With guidance from the original collection, they built on the core of the bequest.

The achievements of the Dixons and the legacy of their example have also served as a catalyst for encouraging other collectors. Individual collections which have become part of the Dixon include Mrs. Warda Stevens Stout's extensive collection of fine porcelain, bequeathed to the Dixon in 1985, Justin and Herta Adler's Pewter Collection, donated in 1991, and, most recently, the Montgomery H.W. Ritchie Collection, twenty-two Impressionist and Post-Impressionist works which expand and complement the Dixons' original bequest. In each case, a dedication to the highest possible quality formed these highly individualized collections, a splendid testimony to the Dixons and the institution they inspired.

There could be no better tribute to the twentieth anniversary of this legacy than the incorporation of the Ritchie Collection into the Dixon's. These two great Englishmen, who made the American South their home, reflect the collecting taste and cultural history which have come to define this part of the country. It is no coincidence that the special strengths of these collections reveal regional preferences that evolved over many generations.

The accomplishments of The Dixon Gallery and Gardens in its twenty short years are phenomenal. From the initial bequest of 33 works of fine art, Board Chairs Eric A. Catmur, S. Herbert Rhea, and Joseph Orgill, III, have expanded the holdings of The Dixon Gallery and Gardens to include over 1,200 works. The Dixon's exquisite gardens provide a peaceful, living counterpart to its splendid collection of fine and decorative arts. Without question, the Dixon has in its short history contributed greatly to a wider appreciation of art and horticulture, while becoming a valuable educational resource for those of all ages and walks of life.

Today, on its twentieth anniversary, The Dixon Gallery and Gardens is a vibrant institution with an enviable future. Unlike many other museums, it does not exist as a monument only to one person or family, but as proof of what a diverse group of dedicated people can accomplish. This publication is a tribute to their vision and to all who have been affiliated with this fine institution.

Hugo and Margaret Dixon, 1947.

The Birth Of The Dixon

ERIC A. CATMUR

Hugo Dixon came into my office one day in November, 1967, and asked me if I would care to become a member of the Hugo Dixon Trust. He explained that he had set up the trust in order to be able to fund some charitable endeavors that he had in mind, and since he and Margaret had no children, the value might be quite substantial after their deaths. He had asked his brother-in-law, William Oates; his friend and lawyer, D. Nelson Adams; Barclay McFadden; Norfleet R. Turner; and me to join with Margaret and himself as the "Committee." He had established the trust with Morgan Guaranty Trust. He told me that the duties were minimal, and about the only thing to be done at that time was for him, as Chairman of the Committee, to write a letter to Morgan Guaranty instructing them to remit some donations or grants to charitable institutions out of the income.

Some time later, he explained that Nelson Adams had suggested to him that the home, gardens and art collection should be kept together and that he might consider leaving them as a museum. Hugo thought this over for awhile (he was not one to make decisions in a hurry) and finally agreed that it would be a fine idea, and it would be a fitting memorial to his wife, Margaret. At that time, he asked me if I would help him with the project, in which case he would ask me to take over as Chairman upon his death.

Besides being a partner with Hugo in the cotton merchandising firm of Geo. H. McFadden & Bro., I had known him for many years, even before he became a member of the McFadden firm, when he was in business with his brother Roger in Dallas. I had heard about him when I was a boy because he and my father were interned as civilian prisoners of war in Germany during the first World War. I was flattered by his offer and accepted with pleasure. Little did I dream that the "minimal duties" Hugo described in 1967 would become almost a full-time job some seven years later!

In the intervening years before his death, Hugo busied himself with planning a gallery room to house his pictures. His concept was to build a state-of-the-art room attached to the residence with perfect lighting and conditions, and a small kitchen area with the usual facilities, with the idea that it would be the place to entertain and show off his pictures. His only problem was the location - should it be to the east, south or west? He had plans drawn for each, but could not find an acceptable one because all would encroach on his much loved garden.

Margaret declined in health over several years and died in the spring of 1974. Hugo, surely grieving, suffered a heart attack shortly thereafter. To cheer Hugo up after he had recuperated, his good friend Abe Plough suggested a trip to Europe. Besides the obligatory visit to the Lido in Paris, they did some serious art dealer shopping. Hugo did the selecting and Abe did the bargaining, and they secured a Cassatt and a Boudin, respectively.

I use the word "secured" purposefully, as Hugo would never allow the purchase to be final until the picture had been shipped and hung in the living room of 4339 Park Avenue and had earned his approval. While in his office on a day in November, he received word that the Cassatt had been delivered. Haywood Nichols, his butler from the time he arrived in Memphis, was unfortunately on vacation, so his nurse-companion drove down to Front Street to pick him up. As they turned homeward, crossing Third Street, the car was hit by another which was running a red light. Although injured, Hugo did not appear to be critically so, and within a few hours was quite coherent. Two days later, however, he went into a decline, perhaps as the result of the shock to his weakened heart, and died on November 25, 1974.

After the funeral, we held the first "Committee" meeting with Nelson Adams, Bill Oates, Norfleet Turner and me in the Chair, the position to which Hugo had appointed me by an amendment to the trust instrument. Joining us now as the executors of Hugo's will were John Martin and Lawson Apperson of the law firm Martin, Tate & Morrow, who represented Hugo in Memphis in certain negotiations, and Gerald Fix of Morgan Guaranty Trust. Abe Plough, as a close friend and confidant of Hugo's, was also present. After the formalities, we discussed the very real responsibilities thrust upon us to carry forward the wishes of Margaret and Hugo. Not only were we to direct the Trustees to distribute the income and to determine the mix of the investments in the trust, but we also had to turn a residence, garden and private art collection into an operating gallery and gardens "open to the public for their enjoyment and pleasure."

In January of 1975 we began to consider our policy options – should we simply turn the residence into a gallery, merely leaving the art pretty well where it had been displayed, or should we follow Hugo's idea of a gallery room to be attached to one side of the residence, or should we decide on a complete state-of-the-art, museum quality wing, fireproofed and climate-controlled to the required professional standards? For the second alternative, Hugo's idea, we had in hand numerous blueprints for an addition to the east, south and west. Hugo could never really make up his mind as to which he preferred, as all would encroach to some extent on his beloved garden. Fortunately, we unanimously chose the third alternative.

To help in this responsibility, I proposed that Abe Plough and Lawson Apperson be elected as additional members (who within days by amendment became "Working Trustees" and the trust changed to a foundation), but Abe demurred, stating that he preferred to remain an advisor, while Lawson accepted. To the present day, Lawson has been a stalwart supporter and advisor, including pro bono publico counselor, and I believe that all of us at the Dixon owe him a deep debt of gratitude. We determined that we would set up a separate non-profit corporation into which we would transfer the physical assets of the estate, which we accomplished by adopting the Charter on May 8, followed by a quit claim deed transfer on December 2, 1975.

Our next step was to decide on a director. There were already a number of applications from highly educated professionals in hand, but they lacked museum experience, so we decided that as difficult as it might be to find one willing to take a chance with a brand new, untried organization, we would only look at applicants who had been either a curator or director at an established art institution. Not unexpectedly, it took many months to find our man.

There was a multitude of matters to be attended to in converting a residence into a gallery. First of all, the Morgan Guaranty Trust, as executor, sent down a couple of officers to take possession and carry out the instructions of the will. Among all the legal procedures to follow, they appointed appraisers to inventory the personal property for probate and tax purposes and then left the rest of the job to us, which turned out to be me, as I had established an office in the master bedroom. There were bequests of furniture and personal possessions to members of Margaret's and Hugo's families that had to be delivered or shipped, and besides the items specified, there was a mass of clothing and personal items that we could not use in the museum business which we distributed to members of the families, I hope judiciously. Over the years Hugo had accumulated drawers full of photographs and snapshots, and to make room I had to weed out those which did not relate to the family or to the house and gardens.

Then there was the question of staffing. We were able in due course to farm out the maids and cooks to good positions elsewhere, retaining Haywood Nichols as the general factotum until he died. Haywood was invaluable; in the early days he alone knew where every switch and water hydrant was. He knew practically everybody and greeted all of us and all of our visitors with a warm welcome.

The gardens were another matter. During Margaret's time she had been the supervisor, seeing that they were always in perfect shape, but when she fell ill her absence was noticeable. Hugo found Alfred Stovick, who had been the head gardener in the McFadden garden in Ellendale, and he held the place together, but we knew that with a garden open to the public we had to have a real, horticulturally knowledgeable staff and so began accumulating trained personnel and searching for a graduate horticulturist as Garden Director.

When Hugo was hospitalized, the family had ordered in security guards from a firm which we retained for a number of years. An electronic alarm system was already in place and was upgraded as we progressed.

There were also a number of architectural or structural changes required. In the Dixons' time the main entrance, which is now the secondary entrance, was down the hill to the northeast of the residence; we viewed this location with apprehension because of the restricted view to the West and decided to move it to a point opposite where Cherry Road dead ends from the North, opposite a path with only a garden gate on the South side of Park Avenue. This entailed designing and building a new formal entrance, a gatehouse and a drive up to the circle in front of the residence. Met Crump, the architect, designed the former, and I the latter. Met also designed the changes from the kitchen and pantry into the back service area. In the course of the next few months, I had the first and then the second of the five upstairs bathrooms taken out to give us more office space. Two more were taken out within a year or two.

A couple of approaches gave us some amusement: hardly had Hugo been buried when a gentleman who said that he was from the Park Commission appeared and asked when they could start cutting the grass. Shortly thereafter, another gentleman tried to convince me that the circumferential drive, not yet paved, would make a fine bicycle stadium.

Sometime in 1974, Florence Snowden told Margaret Catmur that Mrs. Warda Stevens Stout was thinking of donating her collection of German porcelain to a museum or college, and knowing that we were working with Hugo on his plans for a gallery, suggested that Margaret talk to Mrs. Stout, as they were both members of the Memphis Garden Club. This Margaret did, and when Mrs. Stout showed some interest, she arranged a meeting between Mrs. Stout and Hugo. They met one afternoon, and when Margaret had withdrawn, they had a very happy conversation together, with the result that she became interested in the gallery project. This must have taken place in October. They agreed to hold further conversations, or perhaps negotiations, after Hugo returned from Europe.

Tragically, shortly after his return and before they could meet again, he suffered the accident resulting in his death. Hugo's death came as a shock to her, and presumably fearing that the gallery plans would not continue to go forward, she withdrew her interest.

Knowing that the plans would indeed go forward, we searched for a way to revive her interest and found it by asking Abe Plough to visit with her and see if he could sell her on letting us have the porcelain, which would add so much to the existing collection of paintings and the gardens. Abe agreed, and as he did not know Mrs. Stout, Margaret and I introduced them to each other. After viewing the collection, which impressed him (although he would never stop calling it china), Margaret and I left. As they were both somewhat deaf, they got along famously, practically shouting at each other, and after a couple of further visits he even presented her with a set of hearing aids!

After some further talks between all of us we felt we were close to an agreement, so we set a formal lunch meeting in the Dixon dining room. There were present: Mrs. Stout and her daughter, Charlotte Stout Hooker, Abe Plough,

Eric A. Catmur with Mrs. Nancy Glazer, 1986.

Lawson Apperson, Evelyn J. Boyle (who had recently joined our trustee group), Margaret and me. Over an excellent lunch and a good bottle of wine from Hugo's cellar we forged an agreement: that Mrs. Stout would leave the collection to the Dixon, retaining a life interest, provided we would build a suitable separate gallery, further provided that we commence construction no later than December 31, 1976. To seal the accord, Abe said he would contribute $100,000.00 towards the building of such a room, and while announcing this he told Mrs. Stout that he could envision a fine entry door with an inscription above of "The Mrs. Charles B. Stout Gallery." "NO such thing," responded Mrs. Stout, "I bought all of these pieces myself, and it will be 'The Warda Stevens Stout Gallery'!" None of us, except of course Mrs. Stout, realized how important a collection this was, and great credit must be given to Flo Snowden, Margaret Catmur and Abe Plough for their part in securing this truly great asset.

During the years 1956 to 1964, the Dixons had given nine paintings to The Brooks Memorial Art Gallery, retaining a life interest. The paintings were two Pissarros, a Sisley, two Vuillards, a Renoir, a Boudin, a Raeburn, and a Reynolds; they were all fine paintings, and after Hugo had decided on going the way of his own gallery, he regretted the earlier action and would have loved to have had them back, but this proved impossible. When we, the Trustees, took over, we quite naturally had the very same desire, as we sorely needed them to augment the 24 museum-quality paintings that had been left to us in order to present a decent showing when we opened the doors to the public. So our next best move was to approach the Brooks with a request that they loan the nine paintings back to the Dixon for a given period. The Brooks received our request with great sympathy and responded in writing in part as follows:

> "....[we will] cooperate in every way with the (Dixon) Operating Trustees, in helping them organize and bring into fruition an art museum; and that at such time as the Dixon Operating Trustees are organized, staffed and ready to open the Dixon Gallery as a museum that meets acceptable standards, the Brooks Board through the (Board's) Dixon Committee will develop a plan for exhibition of the nine paintings at the Dixon on some loan basis that is mutually agreeable to the parties."

In later negotiations, the loan period for the Brooks paintings was set at two years. To Alexander Dann, the Chairman of the Brooks Board, the Trustees, and the other responsible officials, we must be forever grateful for this most generous boost and act of support.

After the agreement with Mrs. Stout, we began our search for the architect to draw plans for the first museum quality addition, including the Warda Stevens Stout room. I had in mind one of our prominent local people, but a majority of the other trustees wanted a person of national reputation. Evelyn Boyle and Charlotte Stout Hooker had in the meanwhile been elected to our Board of Trustees, and it was Charlotte who searched and found the prospect who fitted that description. It was Edward Vason Jones of Albany, Georgia, above all a connoisseur of antique American furniture and an acknowledged architect of fine colonial Georgian residences. He had been a co-designer of six rooms in the American Wing at the Metropolitan Museum in New York, and he was a member and consulting architect for the Special Committee for the Diplomatic Reception rooms in the State Department, and he held the same positions on the Committee for the Preservation of the White House. For his work he was recognized by the naming of the entrance to the Diplomatic Reception rooms after him, and he was given a Life Fellowship by the Metropolitan, as well as numerous other honors. We had also decided on giving the construction contract to James G. Owen, Jr. of Memphis, a man of the highest reputation as a builder of quality. We had to be very grateful to him for the fine work he produced and his help in some difficult decisions which were to come. His foreman, Sam Tune, was a master craftsman and became our contractor on our second addition.

We commissioned Mr. Jones, and in due course he came in with the plans, which were acceptable as far as the layout was concerned, but not appropriate for a gallery or visual art museum, as each and every gallery was to contain a working fireplace, among other things. Due to the time constraint of getting construction underway by December 31, 1976 and not being able to see eye to eye on what we needed, we had to retire Mr. Jones. With the help of Jimmy Owen we turned to Donald Ray Bingham, who was more of a commercial architect but one who could get things done in a hurry, to take over, which he did successfully, even if it entailed pouring concrete foundations in the freezing December weather! Don Bingham did a fine job for us, so much so that we asked him to do the second, larger addition in 1985.

In the meanwhile we had also been searching for a director, by word of mouth and by advertising in the AAM Journal. We had interviewed a number of prospects without a fit. Then one morning, a somewhat accented voice came on the phone. It was Michael Milkovich, Director of the Museum at the University at Binghamton, New York, and as he sounded like a possibility. I asked him to fly down for an interview. Mike was born in Yugoslavia, later escaping Tito's Communist grip, and was able to get to the United States. He received a higher education at Yale and held several curatorships, ending as the Director in Binghamton. He joined us on January 1, 1976, and set to work organizing the inner workings of a gallery, organizing exhibitions, hiring staff, establishing a membership organization and applying for the American Association of Museums accreditation, which was granted in 1978. His first notable exhibition was *Impressionists in 1877*, in which he assembled a fine collection of works, several from France, to show off and formally open our four new galleries on December 4, 1977.

Thus, by 1976 we had all the pieces that we considered necessary to operate a successful gallery in place: a notable collection (including the nine paintings on a two year loan from the Brooks), a museum quality gallery building under construction, a fine residence and beautiful gardens, a director, and an enthusiastic and supportive Board of Trustees. We believed that we had fulfilled Margaret and Hugo's wishes and were on our way to better and bigger things.

Eric A. Catmur, Chairman Emeritus, served as the first Chairman of the Board of Trustees of
The Dixon Gallery and Gardens.

Photograph by André Kertész, 1952.

Hugo Dixon, 1947. Photograph courtesy of the *Mississippi Valley Collection.*

Hugo Dixon and the English Country House

GEORGE PLUMPTRE

In 1974 the distinguished architectural historian, Olive Cook, wrote about English country house owners of the 18th century:

"They were dominated by a noble zeal for building, for laying out gardens, planting avenues and improving their land and (in striking contrast to ourselves) enhancing instead of destroying nature, achieving a deeply satisfying equilibrium between man and his environment. They patronized living writers, musicians, painters, sculptors and architects, whose art was the part of a process of supply and demand, and not the fringe activity it has since become." [1]

With certain allowances, it is not far-fetched to say that instead of describing the golden age of the country house in England, the author could have been describing Hugo Dixon and his creation of The Dixon Gallery and Gardens in Memphis. Indeed, a fundamental quality of the Dixon is the manner in which it perpetuates the tradition of a country house, garden and art collection created together to make a pleasing aesthetic whole. It was a tradition whose strands were drawn from all over Europe, but whose zenith undoubtedly came in England during the 18th century and a hundred years or so of social and political stability and economic prosperity.

Of course, it would be misleading to suggest that the Dixon home, like other country houses in America, was made in exactly the same mould as those in England. Historically the essential difference was always that the English country house evolved over centuries as a statement of power and establishment, based on the ownership of land, as Mark Girouard explained in his seminal book, *Life in the English Country House*,

"What were English country houses for? They were not originally, whatever they may be now, just large houses in the country in which rich people lived. Essentially they were power houses – the houses of a ruling class... this power was based on land... Land, however, was little use without one or more country houses on it. Land provided the fuel, a country house was the engine which made it effective. It achieved this in a number of ways. It was the headquarters from which land was administered and power organized. It was a show-case in which to exhibit and entertain supporters and good connections... Trophies in the hall, coats of arms over the chimneypieces, books in the library and temples in the park could suggest that he was discriminating, intelligent, bred to rule and brave." [2]

Only a minority of country houses built in America at any time have had a comparable foundation of power by virtue of the ownership of land. It is no coincidence, and a point of direct relevance to the Dixon home, that the one region of the United States where this was true was in the southern states on either side of the Mississippi River, where the European social example and the prosperity of agricultural estates throve. This is hinted at by Clive Aslet in his book, *The American Country House*, as he describes the situation before the surge in country house building in America towards the end of the 19th century,

"Large and costly dwellings had been known before in the United States. Before the Civil War the greatest concentration was seen by those travelers who risked taking a steamboat down the Mississippi; they often expressed admiration for the white-pillared mansions that rose behind alleys of live oaks and azaleas." [3]

From the most prolific period of country house building in America, during the late 19th and early 20th centuries, the majority of houses were built with fortunes made in business, industry or commerce, as exemplified by names such as Vanderbilt, Rockefeller or du Pont. Nonetheless, accepting important differences, the basic inspiration was European, as Aslet confirmed, "European and particularly English houses formed a model in terms of scale, way of life, and sometimes form." Clive Aslet also points out how, by the late 19th century when country houses began to appear in growing numbers in the United States, changes in England meant that there was a recognizeable similarity (or "kinship," as Aslet suggests) between the two countries in why people built country houses and what kind of houses they would be.

[1] Cook, Olive. *The English Country House*. Thames and Hudson and Book Club Associates, 1974.
[2] Girouard, Mark. *Life in the English Country House*. Yale University Press, 1978.
[3] Aslet, Clive. *The American Country House*. Yale University Press, 1984.

"By 1890 the English country house had itself largely outgrown earlier roles. Its meaning had both narrowed and spread. It had narrowed because the country house no longer occupied the position of real power it had held in previous generations; the motive forces were now prestige, tradition, gardening and sport. It had spread because the people who built new houses tended to prefer the illusion to the substance of country life. Land, ownership of which was the traditional basis of the country house, had become considerably less attractive as an investment. To many people it was important to be near a major city. Houses were getting smaller; the suburbs were getting closer. The kinship is closer than it first appears." [4]

And so, this is the country house background into which Hugo Dixon and his creation fits, an Englishman in America, his wealth derived from the strongest mercantile link of all between the two countries, the cotton trade in which he was steeped from an early age. His father and grandfather before him had both been leading figures in the Lancashire cotton industry, and after his education at Charterhouse School in Surrey, founded on the site of a Carthusian monastery, it was almost inevitable that Hugo would follow the family tradition. His early career in Europe with the firm of George H. McFadden & Bro. was interrupted by the First World War and internment by the Germans as a civilian prisoner of war. The most significant step for the future came in 1920, when Hugo arrived in the United States to join his brother Roger, who had established his own cotton merchandising business in Dallas, Texas. In 1936, Hugo moved to join John H. McFadden, Jr. in Houston, and shortly after the firm had moved its headquarters to Memphis in 1939, following the death of McFadden, Hugo was appointed the firm's President.

It is not fanciful to suggest that the establishment of his position perhaps prompted the decision to embark upon building and decorating the country house that was to become increasingly important and rewarding for the rest of his life. But equally significant was his marriage to Margaret Oates Dixon, that had taken place in 1926 in her home town of Memphis. From the very first, the creation of the Dixon was a partnership between the two, and certainly Margaret's contribution to the garden was decisive from the very beginning, when the proposed site from the house was being planned in its surrounding seventeen acres of Tennessee native woodland.

As designed by the Houston architect John Staub and completed in 1941, the Dixon home perpetuated the style of southern country houses; elegant Georgian Revival style with white-pillared entrances on both sides. Inside, the main rooms of the house were planned and decorated by Hugo and Margaret Dixon with an unmistakeably English feel, which has been sensitively retained by the few changes since the Dixon became a gallery. Fine 18th-century English furniture such as the Chippendale commode in the staircase hall, the library chairs and tripod tables in the drawing room and the delightful original chinoiserie decoration of the dining room together promote the atmosphere of a country house, in addition to selected pictures, such as the notable portrait by Sir Joshua Reynolds of Mrs. Richard Crofts. As visitors soon appreciate, however, the most distinguished area of the paintings collection is Impressionism. Eighteenth-century connoisseurs would immediately approve of how Hugo and Margaret Dixon perpetuated a long established tradition in their collecting by combining their admiration for individual works with a desire for the collection to have historical cohesion and identity. As a result, they brought together a group of paintings which illustrate the historical development from the French 19th century Barbizon school represented by Camille Corot, to the views by Eugene Louis Boudin that heralded the main flowering of Impressionism, and specifically work by artists who exhibited at one of the eight Impressionist group shows between 1874 and 1886, among which Edgar Degas' pastel *Dancer Adjusting Her Shoe* is perhaps the most distinguished single work. The Dixons' collecting extended to Pointillism and Post-Impressionism and, fittingly perhaps, the last painting that Hugo Dixon chose before his death in 1974 was the first by an American Impressionist artist to to join the collection, Mary Cassatt's *The Visitor*.

From the decoration and art treasures of the Dixon interiors, one has only to step out from the front door and witness the sweeping vista that extends away across the south lawn to the focal point of the 18th-century sculpture, *Europa and the Bull*, to appreciate the extent to which house and garden were planned as one. Hugo and Margaret Dixon were fortunate in being able to enlist the professional advice of his sister, Hope Crutchfield, a distinguished landscape designer, and together the three of them planned the series of formal vistas through the woodland and the more intimate areas, such as the formal gardens.

During Hugo and Margaret Dixon's lives their home was a source of great pride and happiness that they shared with many others, whether their own friends who enjoyed their private hospitality, or the far wider host of acquaintances to whom they made their home available through their involvement in philanthropic and charitable causes. Without children to become their heirs, their final legacy was in the tradition of many American country house owners, to leave their home endowed and organized for future public enjoyment. Margaret Dixon died in 1974 after suffering from years of declining health, and Hugo only outlived her for a matter of months. Some years before his death, however, he established the Hugo Dixon Trust, with the express purpose that their home would become a gallery and garden open to the public, the details of which are described by Mr. Eric Catmur in his essay, "The Birth of the Dixon."

[4] Ibid.

In the years that have led up to the Dixon's twentieth anniversary in October, 1996, the gallery has been able to expand, both in size and in its collections, adding many works of great distinction through both generous donations and thoughful acquisitions. Equally important for the enjoyment of visitors and the perpetuation of the link with the founders and creative forces, Hugo and Margaret Dixon, the atmosphere of a country home and the *raison d'etre* of the house, garden and art collection survives to continue a long-established and distinguished tradition.

The Dixon Residence

George Plumptre is editor-in-chief of the international magazine *Sotheby's Preview* and the author of many books, including *The Country House Guide* published in 1996.

The Dixon Gallery and Gardens
Tennessee and Texas: Affinities of Taste and History

RICHARD R. BRETTELL

The Dixon Gallery and Gardens opened in 1976 in a home built a generation earlier for Mr. and Mrs. Hugo Dixon by the esteemed architect, John Staub. Although Staub had family in Tennessee – and built his first important house in Knoxville in 1921 – he spent all his working life in Houston, where he was the city's most original and accomplished historicist architect of the 20th century. His specialty was domestic architecture, and he designed homes for many of the most distinguished citizens of Texas. Many of his greatest homes are in Houston and its suburb, River Oaks, but there are also major examples in Dallas, Fort Worth, and Galveston. Staub built three homes in Memphis – the home of Margaret and Hugo Dixon in 1940, the Sprunt house in 1955, and the Brinkley house in 1960.

How and why did Hugo Dixon choose to work with a Texas architect in Memphis? The answer lies in Houston, where Hugo Dixon lived before he arrived in Memphis in 1939. While in Houston, he had acquired a superb site for a house and had already approached John Staub to design it. Although business interests took him permanently to Memphis, forcing him to sell his Houston property (which was later the site of another splendid house by Staub), Dixon remained loyal to the discreet and beautifully crafted architecture and integrated landscape design of his friend. As a result, The Dixon Gallery and Gardens has its permanent home in the first building John Staub designed in Memphis. Interestingly, the Dixon is one of two Staub homes that

Photograph by André Kertész, 1952.

have become public museums. The other, Bayou Bend in Houston's River Oaks, houses the South's finest public collection of American 18th and 19th century decorative arts, and its gardens, like those of the Dixon, are among the public glories of the South.

The ties that bound Hugo Dixon to John Staub were among many that linked Tennessee and Texas between the wars. Because Dallas was also a center for cotton trading, Hugo Dixon's brother lived and worked in Dallas. While there, both brothers met and befriended a fellow Englishman whose principle Texas property is the JA Ranch near Amarillo. The JA Ranch is among the largest and most fabled Texas ranches. Formed in the 1860s as a partnership between John Adair and the legendary Texas cattle driver, Charles Goodnight, Montgomery Ritchie inherited it in the early thirties from his grandmother, Cornelia Adair. Ritchie, like Dixon, came to the United States from England to increase his fortune. Yet, in a manner familiar to other expatriates, each developed a small society of other wealthy English friends who lived in America. This society supplemented and enriched their lives, permitting each of them to escape the rigors of local American society and to connect to their respective roots. The Dixon brothers and their friend Montie Ritchie met many times, played polo together, and discussed everything from mutual business interests to the shared passion of Montie Ritchie and Hugo Dixon for the arts.

The homes of both Hugo Dixon and Montie Ritchie were filled with American and English furniture, porcelain, "Oriental" carpets, and modern French paintings and drawings. Like many English collectors of their generation, they loved the work of the Impressionists and Post-Impressionists. Both were also interested in comparable American artists, including expatriates like John Singer Sargent and Mary Cassatt. Ritchie never needed to build a house on the JA Ranch. His grandmother, Cornelia Adair, had already commissioned an Edwardian stone house with porches and rose gardens at the end of a long dirt road. The interior of the house looked a good deal like that of the home we now call the Dixon – a Renoir seascape poised on the wall over an English sideboard, its polished top reflecting the subtle colors and contours of Chinese porcelain. How perfectly at home this ensemble would have looked in Staub's house for Hugo Dixon. Realizing that keeping magnificent works of art in perpetuity on the walls of a remote ranch in Texas is a difficult task for any contemporary family, the Ritchie Family decided to share their greatest treasures with the public. What better place for their collection could be imagined than the Dixon?

This publication is the first to celebrate the marriage of the Dixon Collection and the Ritchie Collection and to build one of the many bridges between Texas and Tennessee that Dixon himself started. There are enough connections to fill a book, but a simple list will suffice here: the "pairs" of works – one Dixon, the other Ritchie – by Boudin, Pissarro, Marquet, and Chagall; the rhymes of the expatriates, Sargent and Cassatt; the addition of two works by Monet from the Ritchie Collection to the Dixon Collection that includes a painting by Monet's American student and son-in-law, Theodore Earl Butler; the home provided at the Dixon for a wonderful painting by the greatest of all Neo-Impressionist painters, Georges Seurat, in a group of pictures by many of his major followers and colleagues.

What one celebrates at the anniversary of the Dixon is the steady and intelligent growth of an institution on a firm financial base – and a growth that Hugo Dixon himself would have felt to be perfectly consistent with his aims in creating the first "house/ garden" opened permanently to the public in Memphis. Fortunately, Montie Ritchie and his daughter, Cornelia Bivins, can celebrate the occasion with their new friends in Memphis, and Montie can remember the many hours he spent with his old friend, Hugo Dixon. The third man in this triumvirate, John Staub, who like Hugo Dixon is no longer living, would surely have shared the pleasure of knowing that the house and gardens he created in Memphis for a childless couple is now enjoyed by thousands of Memphians and their guests every year. The connections between Texas and Tennessee achieve their highest level at The Dixon Gallery and Gardens, and all of us who love – and live in – the Lone Star State need to visit Memphis to see just how "we all" have benefited from the taste and discrimination of two English expatriates – one, Hugo Dixon, to Tennessee and the other, Montie Ritchie, to Texas. How at home their treasures look in John Staub's understated Georgian house with its equally understated Georgian addition. The glories of Tennessee's nature make the Dixon's garden setting even more perfect.

Richard R. Brettell, an independant scholar and consultant, has been affiliated with The Dixon Gallery and Gardens since 1979 when he prepared the exhibition catalogue *Homage to Camille Pissaro: The Last Years, 1880-1903.*

Photograph by André Kertész, 1952.

André Kertész
1894-1985

The Dixon Residence and Gardens

André Kertész is generally considered to be one of the most important photographers of the 20th century. Born in Budapest in 1894, Kertész traveled to Paris in 1925, where he found both an intriguing host of subjects and a community of artists and critics who welcomed his work. In the 1920s and 30s, the enormous popularity of postwar mass publications facilitated his ability to begin selling photos to French and German illustrated magazines.[1] His involvement in a close circle of Hungarian friends in Paris introduced him to some of the most significant figures in abstract painting, such as Piet Mondrian and Fernand Léger. Kertész in the 1930s began to exhibit his works, often showing with experimentalist photographers like Laszlo Moholy-Nagy and Man Ray, although his own work was far more naturalistic.[2]

Kertész took an opportunity offered to him in 1935 to work for Keystone Studios in New York, and abruptly his career and art changed with his new location. From his arrival in New York in 1936 through the early 1940s, Kertész had a difficult time working in the highly commercial, competitive world of American photography, which did not receive his work with the friendly acclaim he had received in Paris in the 1920s.[3] He continued to work as a photographer for various New York weekly magazines, among them *Harper's Bazaar, Town and Country*, and *Vogue*. The struggle in his professional career and the war in Europe, which focused negative emotions toward immigrants such as himself, seemed to be reflected in his personal work.[4]

Kertész was offered a contract in 1946 to work exclusively for *House and Garden* magazine, for whom he worked until 1962. *House and Garden* allowed him to travel extensively across the United States, primarily photographing interiors and architectural elements. The gardens of Hugo and Margaret Dixon's estate were photographed by Kertész in April of 1952 as part of an assignment for the magazine. The photographs included in this publication are part of nearly a dozen Kertész images of the Dixon grounds which capture both the sweeping vistas and intimate qualities of Hugo and Margaret's private gardens. In 1962, at the age of sixty-eight, Kertész retired fully from *House and Garden* to concentrate on his own art.

André Kertész is a photographer whose work has been increasingly recognized in recent years in the art communities of the United States and Europe. In 1985, just before his death, a major retrospective exhibition of Kertész's work opened at The Art Institute of Chicago and The Metropolitan Museum of Art, New York, which closely examined the life and work of this important artist.

1. Sandra S. Phillips. "André Kertész: The Years in Paris," in *André Kertész: Of Paris and New York*. Chicago: Thames and Hudson, 1985, pp. 17-55.

2. Ibid.

3. David Travis. "Kertész and his Contemporaries in Germany and France," in *André Kertész: Of Paris and New York*. Chicago: Thames and Hudson, 1985, pp. 57-91.

4. Weston J. Naef. "André Kertész: The Making of an American Photographer," in *André Kertész: Of Paris and New York*. Chicago: Thames and Hudson, 1985, pp. 95-124.

Europa and the Bull

Unknown Artist, British, 18th century

Marble
101 x 61 x 41 1/4 in. 256.5 x 154.9 x 104.8 cm.

PROVENANCE:
Captain John Fielden, Grimston Park, Tadcaster, York, England

T. Crowther & Sons, London

Mr. and Mrs. Hugo Dixon, 1962

The Dixon Gallery and Gardens, 1976

Collection of The Dixon Gallery and Gardens,
Bequest of Mr. and Mrs. Hugo Dixon, 1975.31

THE DIXON GALLERY AND GARDENS

Abbreviations

Alexandre
    Alexandre, Arséne. *A.-F. Cals* . Paris: Georges Petit, 1900.
Bataille
    Bataille, M.-L. and Georges Wildenstein. *Berthe Morisot: Catalogue des peintures, pastels, et aquarelles*. Paris, 1961.
Bouin-Luce
    Bouin-Luce, Jean and Denise Bazetoux. *Maximilien Luce: Catalogue raisonné de l'oeuvre peint*. Vol. 2, Paris: Editions JBL, 1986.
Breeskin
    Breeskin, A. D. *Mary Cassatt - A Catalogue Raisonné of the Oils, Pastels, Watercolors, and Drawings*. Washington, DC, 1970.
Compin
    Compin, Isabelle. *H. E. Cross*. Paris, 1964.
Dauberville
    Dauberville, Jean and Henry. *Bonnard: Catalogue raisonné de l'oeuvre peint*. Vol. II, Paris, 1965-1974.
Daulte
    Daulte, François. *Alfred Sisley, Catalogue raisonné de l'oeuvre peint*. Lausanne,1959.
    Daulte, François. *Auguste Renoir, Catalogue raisonné de l'oeuvre peint*. Lausanne, 1971.
De Hauke
    De Hauke, C. M. *Seurat et son oeuvre*. Paris, 1961.
Dieterle
    Dieterle, Jean. *Corot, Troisième supplément "L'oeuvre de Corot" par A. Robaut et Moreau-Nélaton*. Paris: Quatre Chemins-éditart, 1974.
Fantin-Latour
    Fantin-Latour, Madame Henri. *Catalogue de l'oeuvre complet de Fantin-Latour (1849-1904)*. Paris: Henri Floury, 1911.
Graves and Cronin
    Graves, A. and W. V. Cronin. *A History of the Works by Joshua Reynolds*. Vol. I-IV, London, 1901.
Guillon-Lafaille
    Guillon-Lafaille, Fanny. *Raoul Dufy: Catalogue raisonné des aquarelles, gouaches, et pastels*. Paris, 1981.
Hediard
    Hediard, Germain. *Fantin-Latour, Catalogue de l'oeuvre lithographique*. Paris, 1900.
Hefting
    Hefting, Victorine. *Jongkind, sa vie, son oeuvre, son epoque*. Paris, 1975.
Lafaille
    Lafaille, Maurice. *Raoul Dufy, Catalogue raisonné de l'oeuvre peint*. Vol. III, Geneva, 1973.
Lemoisne
    Lemoisne, P. A. *Peintures et pastels*. Paris: Brame and Hauke, Arts et Métiers Graphiques, 1946.
Lund Humphries
    Lund Humphries. *Henry Moore Sculpture and Drawings 1921-48*. London, 1990.
Maeght
    Maeght Editeur. *Catalogue de l'oeuvre de Georges Braque, Peintures 1924-1927*. Paris, 1961.
Miquel
    Miquel, Pierre. *Eugéne Isabey (1803-1886) La marine au XIXe siecle*. Maurs-la-Jolie, 1980.
Orienti
    Orienti, Sandra. *The Complete Paintings of Cézanne*. Harmondsworth: Penguin Books, 1970.
Pétridès
    Pétridès, Paul. *L'oeuvre complet de Maurice Utrillo*. Vol. II, Paris, 1959.
Prendergast
    Clark, Carol, Nancy Mowll Mathews and Gwendolyn Owens. *Maurice Brazil Prendergast, Charles Prendergast, A Catalogue Raisonné*. Williamstown: Williams College Museum of Art, 1990.
Robaut
    Robaut, Alfred. *L'oeuvre de Corot: Catalogue raisonné et illustré*. Vol. II, Paris: H. Floury, 1905.
Russoli
    Russoli, Franco. *L'Opera Completa di Degas*. Milan: Rizzoli Editore, 1970.
Schmit
    Schmit, Robert and Manuel. *Stanislas Lepine: Catalogue raisonné de l'oeuvre peint*. Paris:Éditions Galerie Schmit, 1993.
    Schmit, Robert. *Eugene Boudin, 1824-1898*. Vol. III, Paris: Éditions Galerie Schmit,1973.
Soutine
    Tuchman, Maurice, Esti Dunow and Klaus Perls. *Chaim Soutine (1893-1943): Catalogue Raisonné*. Cologne, 1993.
Venturi
    Pissarro, Ludovic Rodo and Lionello Venturi. *Camille Pissarro - son art, son oeuvre*. Paris, 1939.
    Venturi, Lionello. *Cezanne, son art - son oeuvre*. Vol. I, Paris: Paul Rosenberg Éditeur, 1936.
Wildenstein
    Wildenstein, Georges. *Paul Gauguin: Catalogue raisonné*. Vol. I, Paris, 1964.
    Wildenstein, Daniel. *Claude Monet, Biographie et catalogue raisonné*. Vol. I-II, Lausanne and Paris: L'Institut, 1974-1979.

Sir Joshua Reynolds
(English, 1723-1792)

Portrait of Mrs. Richard Crofts

Oil on canvas
50 3/4 x 45 in.   129 x 114.3 cm.
Painted in 1775

PROVENANCE:
Sale, Christie's, London, June 29, 1889
Sale, Christie's, London, February 22, 1890
Sebright Family, Besford, Worchestershire, England
Sir Edgar Sebright, England, 1908
Thomas Agnew & Sons, London
Mme. Jacques Balsan, New York
M. Knoedler & Co., Inc., New York
John H. McFadden, Jr., Memphis, Tennessee
Philadelphia Museum of Art, 1956
Sale, Parke-Bernet, Property of the Philadelphia Museum of Art, February 29, 1956, no. 39
Mr. and Mrs. Hugo Dixon, 1956
The Dixon Gallery and Gardens, 1976

EXHIBITED:
London, *Winter Exhibition of Works by the Old Masters*, Royal Academy, 1908, no. 154.

SELECTED REFERENCES:
William Cotton. *Sir Joshua Reynolds, Notes and Observations on Pictures.* London, 1859, pp. 84-85.
Sir Walter Armstrong. *Sir Joshua Reynolds.* London, 1900, p. 201.
Ellis K. Waterhouse. *Reynolds.* New York: Phaidon, 1941, pp. 65-66.

CATALOGUE RAISONNE:
Graves and Cronin, Vol. I, p. 213; Vol. IV, facing p. 1472
This work will be included in the forthcoming Reynolds catalogue raisonné being prepared
  by David Mannings at The University of Aberdeen, Scotland.

Collection of The Dixon Gallery and Gardens, Bequest of Mr. and Mrs. Hugo Dixon, 1975.2

Giacomo Guardi
(Italian, 1764-1835)

View of Venice, the Dogana and Santa Maria della Salute

Gouache on paper
5 7/8 x 9 3/8 in. 14.8 x 23.6 cm.
Executed circa 1782-1790

PROVENANCE:
Marlborough Fine Art, Ltd., London

Mrs. Rosalee Cohn, 1956

The Dixon Gallery and Gardens, 1976

EXHIBITED:
London, Giacomo Guardi - Views of Venice, Marlborough Fine Arts, 1956, no. 14.

Collection of The Dixon Gallery and Gardens, Gift of Mrs. Rosalee Cohn, 1976.15

Paul Delaroche
(French, 1797-1856)

Sleeping Woman

Signed and dated lower left: P. Delaroche 1825
Black and red chalk on paper
5 3/4 x 8 1/8 in.   14.5 x 20.5 cm.

PROVENANCE:
Schaeffer Galleries, New York

Louise Richards, Cleveland, Ohio, 1974

Ms. Anne Lockhardt, Memphis, Tennessee, 1981

The Dixon Gallery and Gardens, 1987

EXHIBITED:
Cleveland, Art for Collectors, Cleveland Museum of Art, 1974.

Collection of The Dixon Gallery and Gardens, Gift of Mr. and Mrs. William T. Arthur, Jr.,
Mr. and Mrs. Peter R. Beasley, Mr. and Mrs. Keith W. Brown, Mr. and Mrs. F. Friedgen
in honor of Dr. and Mrs. George A. Coors, 1987.105

Sir Henry Raeburn
(British, 1756-1823)

Lady Don with Her Granddaughter, Mary Don

Oil on canvas
49 3/4 x 39 1/4 in. 126.4 x 99.7 cm.
Painted circa 1794

PROVENANCE:

Lady Milbank (Alexina Harriet Elizabeth Don), Barningham Park, Barnard Castle, England

Sir Frederick Acclom Milbank, Baronet, Barningham Park, Barnard Castle, England, circa 1880

Dowager Lady Milbank, Barningham Park, Barnard Castle, England

Sale, Christie's, London, Aird Collection, December 19,1945

Scott and Fowles, New York

Sale, Christie's, London, July 25, 1952

McFadden Family, Philadelphia

Philadelphia Museum of Art, circa 1956

Sale, Parke Bernet, Property of the Philadelphia Museum of Art, Feb. 19, 1956, no. 38

Billy Rose, New York

Sale, Sotheby's, London, Fine 18th and 19th Century Paintings, July 12, 1967, no. 83

Lyman Stansky, New York, 1967

Mr. and Mrs. Hugo Dixon, 1967

The Dixon Gallery and Gardens, 1976

EXHIBITED:

York, England, Yorkshire Fine Art Institute, 1880.

Collection of The Dixon Gallery and Gardens, Bequest of Mr. and Mrs. Hugo Dixon, 1975.18

Jean-Baptiste-Camille Corot
(French, 1796-1875)

The Paver of the Chailly Road, Fontainebleau

Signed lower left: Corot
Oil on canvas
11 3/4 x 16 3/4 in. 29.9 x 42.5 cm.
Painted circa 1830-35

PROVENANCE:

Cibiel and Chauchard, Paris, 1892

Dr. P. Lannelongue Collection

Sale, Vente P. Lannelongue, Paris, December 11, 1912, no. 31

Private Collection, London

Arthur Tooth & Sons, Ltd., London

Mr. and Mrs. Hugo Dixon, 1973

The Dixon Gallery and Gardens, 1976

EXHIBITED:

London, Recent Acquisitions XXV, Arthur Tooth & Sons, Ltd., 1970, no. 6.
London, Paris-Londres, Arthur Tooth & Sons, Ltd., 1972, no. 14.
Tokyo, J.B. Camille Corot Exhibition, Odakyu Grared Gallery, traveled to: Navio Museum of Art, Osaka;
   The Miyazaki Prefectural Museum, Miyazaki; Sogo Museum of Art, Yokohama, 1989-1990, p. 142, no. 8.
New Hampshire, Corot to Monet: The Rise of Landscape Painting in France, The Currier Gallery of Art, traveled to:
   IBM Gallery of Science and Art, New York; Dallas Museum of Art, Dallas; High Museum of Art, Atlanta, 1991-1992.

SELECTED REFERENCES:
Pierre Miquel. Paysage et societé 1800-1900: L'ecole de la nature. Maurs-la-Jolie, 1985, p. 158.

CATALOGUE RAISONNE:
Dieterle 10

Collection of The Dixon Gallery and Gardens, Bequest of Mr. and Mrs. Hugo Dixon, 1975.25

Louis Gabriel Eugène Isabey

(French, 1803-1886)

Portrait of the Artist's Wife, Laura Lebreton

Inscribed with stamp lower right: Vente Isabey
Oil on canvas
21 3/4 x 18 in.   55.4 x 46.3 cm.
Painted circa 1845

PROVENANCE:
Sale, Isabey, Paris, March 30-31, 1887, no. 67

Galerie Georges Petit, 1887

Sale, Hotel Drouot, 1934

Private Collection, France

Galerie Hopkins-Thomas, Paris

The Dixon Gallery and Gardens, 1993

SELECTED REFERENCES:
Miquel, Pierre. Eugene Isabey, Le paysage francais: L'ecole de la nature. Vol. 9,
  Maurs-la-Jolie, 1985, pp. 69 and 98.

CATALOGUE RAISONNE:
Miquel 1024

Collection of The Dixon Gallery and Gardens, Gift of the Arthur F. and Alice E. Adams Charitable Foundation -
Mr. and Mrs. Henry Cauley Clark, 1993.12

Charles-Emile Jacque
(French, 1813-1894)

The Alchemist

Signed lower right: Ch. Jacque
Oil on canvas
18 1/4 x 22 1/16 in.   46.5 x 56.0 cm.
Painted circa 1850

PROVENANCE:
Mrs. Ruth S. Colliins
Mrs. E. D. Connell and Mrs. James Lynn
The Dixon Gallery and Gardens, 1992

Collection of The Dixon Gallery and Gardens, Gift of Mrs. E. D. Connell and Mrs. James Lynn, 1992.1

Johan Barthold Jongkind
(Dutch/French School, 1819-1891)

The Village of Saint-Parize

Signed lower right: Jongkind and inscribed lower left: St. Parize 14 Septembre, 1861
Watercolor on paper
10 1/4 x 17 5/8 in.   26.0 x 44.7 cm.

PROVENACE:
Sale, Hotel Drouot, Tableaux, esquisses, etudes et aquarelles par feu, J. B. Jongkind, Dec. 7-8, 1891, no. 93
Galerie Schmit, Paris
Mr. and Mrs. Hugo Dixon, 1972
The Dixon Gallery and Gardens, 1976

CATALOGUE RAISONNE:
Hefting 224

Collection of The Dixon Gallery and Gardens, Bequest of Mr. and Mrs. Hugo Dixon, 1975.22

Henri Fantin-Latour
(French, 1836-1904)

Still Life

Signed and dated lower center: Fantin 69
Oil on canvas
18 x 14 1/2 in.   45.7 x 36.8 cm.

PROVENANCE:
Edwin Edwards, London

A. M. Haseltine, London

Mrs. Tempelaere, France

Lawson Peacock, London

Williams & Son, London

The Lefevre Gallery, London

Ian MacNicol, Glasgow

Sale, Galerie George Petit, Paris, 1920

Sale, Christie's, London, July 1949

Scott & Fowles, New York, 1952

Mr. and Mrs. Hugo Dixon, 1952

The Dixon Gallery and Gardens, 1976

CATALOGUE RAISONNE:
Fantin-Latour 326
This work will be included in the forthcoming Fantin-Latour catalogue raisonné
  being produced by Hector Brame and Jean Lorenceau.

Collection of The Dixon Gallery and Gardens, Bequest of Mr. and Mrs. Hugo Dixon, 1975.29

Claude Monet

(French, 1840-1926)

Village Street

Inscribed with estate stamp lower right: Claude Monet (Lugt 1819b)
Oil on canvas
16 1/4 x 25 in. 41.3 x 63.4 cm.
Painted circa 1869-71

PROVENANCE:
Michel Monet, Giverny

A. & R. Ball, Montreal, 1940

Van Diemen-Lilienfeld Galleries, New York

Montgomery H. W. Ritchie, Clarendon, Texas, 1952

Cornelia Ritchie Bivins, Amarillo, Texas

The Dixon Gallery and Gardens, 1996

EXHIBITED:
Montreal Museum of Fine Arts, Oct. 4-29, 1950, no. 21.
Dallas, Texas, Impressionist and Modern Masters in Dallas,
  Dallas Museum of Art, 1989, no. 62.

CATALOGUE RAISONNE:
Wildenstein 243
This work will be included in the forthcoming Monet catalogue raisonné
  being produced by Bea Rehders, Paris.

Collection of The Dixon Gallery and Gardens,
Gift of Cornelia Ritchie Bivins and Museum Purchase, 1996.2.6

Auguste Rodin
(French, 1840-1917)

Young Girl with Flowers in Her Hair

Bronze
19 1/4 x 13 1/2 x 9 1/2 in. 49.0 x 34.3 x 24.1 cm.
Executed circa 1868
Cast 6/12, Coubertin Foundry

PROVENANCE:
B. Gerald Cantor Art Foundation

The Dixon Gallery and Gardens, 1987

EXHIBITED:
Memphis, The Passion of Rodin: Sculpture from the B. Gerald Cantor Collection,
  The Dixon Gallery and Gardens and Lakeview Museum of Arts and Science, 1988.

Collection of The Dixon Gallery and Gardens,
Gift of the Iris and B. Gerald Cantor Foundation, 1987.3

Jean-Baptiste Carpeaux
(French, 1827-1875)

Daphnis and Chloe

Signed and dated top of base: J. B. Carpeaux, 1875
Terracotta
26 1/2 x 11 1/8 in.   66.25 x 11.1 cm.

PROVENANCE:

Wildenstein & Company, Inc., New York

Mr. and Mrs. Hugo Dixon, 1966

The Dixon Gallery and Gardens, 1976

EXHIBITED:

New York, Carpeaux, Wildenstein & Company, Inc., 1965-66, no. 21.
Los Angeles, The Romantics to Rodin: French 19th Century Sculpture
   from North American Collections, Los Angeles County Museum of Art, 1980-81, no. 43.

Collection of The Dixon Gallery and Gardens, Bequest of Mr. and Mrs. Hugo Dixon, 1975.16

MEISSEN
Decorated by Johann Gregor Höroldt (German, 1696-1775)

"Oppenheimer" Tankard

Unmarked
Hard-paste porcelain
7 7/8 x 3 3/4 x 5 1/4 in.   20.0 x 9.5 x 13.3 cm.
Executed circa 1722

PROVENANCE:
Marren Soren Fatter, Denmark, 1752

M.S.S.Z., Denmark, 1859

Margaret and Dr. Franz Oppenheimer, Berlin and Copenhagen

Dr. Fritz Mannheimer, Amsterdam

H. E. Backer, London, 1952

J. J. Klejman, New York

Ralph Wark, Hendersonville, North Carolina

Warda Stevens Stout, 1959

The Dixon Gallery and Gardens, 1985

SELECTED REFERENCES:
Ludwig Schnorr von Carolsfeld. Sammlung Margaret und Franz Oppenheimer, n.d., no. 126.
Mannheimer Sammlung Sales Catalogue. Amsterdam, 1952, p. 34, no. 313.
Ralph Wark. "Johann Gregor Horoldt 1696-1775," Keramik-Freunde der Schweitz no. 39, 1957, fig. 23.
Siegfried Ducret. "Die Arbeitsmethoden Johann Gregor Horoldts," Keramik Freunde der Schweitz no. 39, 1957, fig. 57.
G. Ryland and Cleo Scott. Antique Porcelain Digest. Newport, 1961, p. 189, no. 190.

Collection of The Dixon Gallery and Gardens, Gift of Warda Stevens Stout, 1985.DA.46

MEISSEN
Modeled by Johann Joachim Kändler (German, 1706-1775)

Harlequin and Columbine Dancing

Inscribed with crossed swords in underglaze blue
Hard-paste porcelain
8 5/8 x 7 x 4 1/2 in.   21.8 x 17.6 x 11.3 cm.
Executed circa 1744

PROVENANCE:
Baron Max von Goldschmidt-Rothschild, Frankfurt am Main

Rosenberg and Stiebel, New York

Warda Stevens Stout, 1956

The Dixon Gallery and Gardens, 1985

SELECTED REFERENCES:
Ralph Wark. "Museums and the Fine Arts in the United States," Keramik-Freunde der Schweitz no. 45, 1959, pl. VII, fig. 25.
G. Ryland and Cleo Scott. Antique Porcelain Digest. Newport, 1961, p. 191, no. 293.
Warda Stevens Stout. Mrs. C. B. Stout Collection of Early Meissen Porcelain ca. 1708-1750.
  Memphis: Brooks Memorial Art Gallery, 1966, no. 84.

Collection of The Dixon Gallery and Gardens, Gift of Warda Stevens Stout, 1985.DA.52

HÖCHST

Modeled by Johann Peter Melchior (German, 1742-1825)

The Adorned Sleeper

Inscribed with crowned wheel mark in underglaze blue
Hard-paste porcelain
6 1/2 x 7 1/4 in.   16.4 x 18.4 cm.
Executed circa 1770

PROVENANCE:

Maria von Steinmeister, Königstein

Adolf von Brüning, Königstein

Fritz Weber, Frankfurt am Main

Warda Stevens Stout, 1950

The Dixon Gallery and Gardens, 1985

SELECTED REFERENCES:
Kurt Röder and Michael Oppenheim. Das Höchster Porzellan auf der Jahrtausendausstellung
    in Mainz 1925. Mainz, 1930, no. 68.

Collection of The Dixon Gallery and Gardens, Gift of Warda Stevens Stout, 1985.DA.311

O. H. Perron
(French, 19th century)

Art Nouveau pitcher

Pewter
9 3/4 x 6 1/2 x 6 in. 24.7 x 16.4 x 15.1 cm.
Executed circa 1896

PROVENANCE:

Dr. and Mrs. Justin Adler, Memphis, Tennessee

The Dixon Gallery and Gardens, 1991

Collection of The Dixon Gallery and Gardens,
Gift of Dr. and Mrs. Justin Adler, 1991.DA.10.45

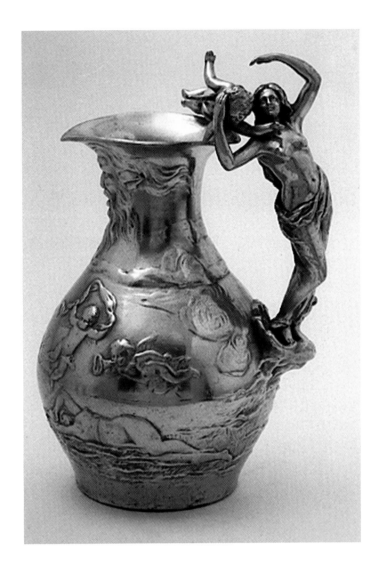

Lidded Tureen
Mason's Ironstone Dinner Service, English, circa 1835

Stoneware
10 x 12 x 12 in.   25.4 x 30.4 x 30.4 cm.

PROVENANCE:

Mr. Jack Smith, Memphis, Tennessee

The Dixon Gallery and Gardens, 1985

Collection of The Dixon Gallery and Gardens, Gift of Mr. Jack Smith, 1995. 2.10

Adolphe-Félix Cals
(French, 1810-1880)

Mother Boudoux at Her Window

Signed and dated lower left: Cals Honfleur 1876
Oil on canvas
23 1/8 x 18 3/4 in.   58.8 x 47.7 cm.

PROVENANCE:

Auguste Godin, Paris, circa 1900

Private Collection, Paris

Galerie Delestre, Paris, circa 1975

The Dixon Gallery and Gardens, 1977

EXHIBITED:
Paris, Third Impressionist Exhibition, 1877, catalogue no. 13, p. 4.
Paris, Exhibition A.-F. Cals, Galerie Georges Petit, 1901, catalogue no. 148.
Paris, A.-F. Cals, 1810-1880, Galerie Delestre, 1975, catalogue no. 31.

SELECTED REFERENCES:
C. S. Moffett and R. Berson. The New Painting: Impressionism 1874-1886.
  The Fine Arts Museums of San Francisco, 1986, p. 21, fig. 4.

CATALOGUE RAISONNÉ:
Alexandre 210

Collection of The Dixon Gallery and Gardens, Museum Purchase, 1977.3

Alfred Sisley
(French 1839/40-1899)

The Seine at Billancourt

Signed lower right: Sisley
Oil on canvas
15 x 21 1/2 in.   38.2 x 54.6 cm.
Painted circa 1877-78

PROVENANCE:

Madame Pierre Colle

Galerie Pétridès, Paris

Arthur Tooth & Sons, London

Alex Reid & Lefevre Gallery, London

Montgomery H. W. Ritchie, Clarendon, Texas, 1959

The Dixon Gallery and Gardens, 1996

EXHIBITED:
Dallas, Texas, Impressionist and Modern Masters in Dallas,
  Dallas Museum of Art, 1989, catalogue no. 104.

CATALOGUE RAISONNÉ:
This work will be included in the forthcoming supplement
  to the Sisley catalogue raisonné being prepared by Francois Daulte.

Collection of The Dixon Gallery and Gardens, Gift of Montgomery H. W. Ritchie, 1996.2.15

Charles François Daubigny
(French, 1817-1878)

Church at Auvers, Twilight

Inscribed with estate stamp lower left and lower right: CD
Oil on canvas
32 3/8 x 60 1/2 in.   82.2 x 153.7 cm.
Painted circa 1875-1878

PROVENANCE:

Karl Daubigny (artist's son)

Drouot Auction House

Sale, Daubigny Estate, Paris, May 6-8, 1878, lot no. 363

Charles Sedelmeyer, Paris, circa 1893

Mr. and Mrs. Norman Hirschl, New York

The Dixon Gallery and Gardens, 1978

EXHIBITED:

New York, Corot and His Contemporaries, Hirschl & Adler Galleries, Inc., 1965,
  catalogue no. 22, illustrated as Landscape with House Near Pontoise, 1866.

Collection of The Dixon Gallery and Gardens,
Gift of Mr. and Mrs. Norman Hirschl, 1978.2

Jean François Raffaelli
(French, 1850-1924)

The Place D'Italie, After the Rain

Signed and inscribed lower right: J. F. Raffaelli La Place d'Italie Apres la Pluie-Paris Mai 1877
Oil on canvas
15 x 22 1/4 in.   38.1 x 56.5 cm.

PROVENANCE:
Private Collection, Paris

Hirschl and Adler Galleries, Inc., New York

The Dixon Gallery and Gardens, 1984

Collection of The Dixon Gallery and Gardens, Museum Purchase, 1984

Alfred Sisley
(French, 1839/40-1899)

The Quay of the Seine During Snow Season

Signed and dated lower right: Sisley 79
Oil on canvas
14 3/4 x 18 in.   37.5 x 45.8 cm.

PROVENANCE:

Jacques Doubourg, Paris

Marlborough Fine Arts, Ltd., London

Private Collection, London, circa 1959

W. G. Wing, Bangor, Maine

Hirschl and Adler Galleries, Inc., New York

The Dixon Gallery and Gardens, 1979

EXHIBITED:
London, Pissarro-Sisley, Marlborough Fine Art, Ltd., 1955, catalogue no. 34.
London, XIXth and XXth Century European Masters,
  Marlborough Fine Art, Ltd., 1955, catalogue no. 73.
London, Exhibition of French Masters of the Nineteenth and Twentieth Century,
  Ohana Gallery, 1957, catalogue no. 46.

CATALOGUE RAISONNÉ:
Daulte (1959) 310

Collection of The Dixon Gallery and Gardens, Museum Purchase, 1979.3

Jean-Louis Forain
(French, 1852-1931)

At the Café

Signed lower left: L. Forain
Watercolor and gouache on paper
12 7/8 x 10 in.   33.3 x 25.8 cm.
Executed circa 1879

PROVENANCE:

Palais Galliera, 1972

Lefevre Gallery, London

Private Collection, Switzerland

E. J. Van Wisselingh and Company, Amsterdam

Private Collection, Holland

Galerie Hopkins-Thomas, Paris

The Dixon Gallery and Gardens, 1993

EXHIBITED:
Paris, Quatrieme exposition de peinture, 1879, no. 86.
Amsterdam, Maitres Francais du XIXme et XXme siecles, E.J. Van Wisselingh & Co., 1975, catalogue no. 13.
Washington, DC, The New Painting - Impressionism 1874-1886, National Gallery of Art, traveled to:
  San Francisco, The Fine Arts Museum of San Francisco, M. H. de Young Memorial Museum, 1986, catalogue no. 77, p. 282.
Osaka, Utrillo et les Artistes de Montmartre, traveled to: Kyoto, Japan; Tokyo, Japan, 1990, catalogue no. 29.
Amsterdam, Jean-Louis Forain: The Impressionist Years, Van Gogh Museum, traveled to:
  Glasgow, The Burrell Collection; Lausanne, Fondation de L'Hermitage; Paris, Galerie Hopkins-Thomas, 1995, catalogue no. 7.

SELECTED REFERENCES:
Musée Americain de Giverny, Lasting Impressions, American Painters in France, 1865-1915,
  Terra Foundation for the Arts, 1992, p. 238.

Collection of The Dixon Gallery and Gardens, Museum Purchase, 1993.7.2

Edgar Degas
(French, 1834-1917)

Ballet Scene

Signed lower left: Degas
Oil on paper laid on wood panel
20 x 22 5/8 in.   50.8 x 57.5 cm.
Painted in 1880

PROVENANCE:
Galerie Georges Petit, 3me Vente Atelier Degas, March 8-9, 1919, lot no. 10

Madame J. Danthon, Paris

Sale, Hotel Drouot, Collection de Madame J. Danthon, Catalogue des Tableaux Modernes Aquarelles et Dessins,
  May 24, 1933, lot no. 23, illustrated p. 18

Mouradian-Vallotton, Paris

Mr. and Mrs. Walter Ross, New York

Sale, Parke-Bernet Galleries, Modern Paintings and Sculptures from the Collection of
  Mr. and Mrs. Walter Ross, New York, October 21, 1964, lot no. 26

Sara Lee Corporation

The Dixon Gallery and Gardens, 1991

EXHIBITED:
Paris, Tableaux, Pastels et Dessins par Edgar Degas,
  Galerie Georges Petit, 1919, catalogue no. 10, p. 14.
New York, Modern Paintings and Sculptures from the Collection of Mr. and Mrs. Walter Ross,
  Parke-Bernet Galleries, October 15-21, 1964.
Palo Alto, California, Stanford University, 1969.
Chicago, The Art Institute of Chicago, 1973.
Dayton, Ohio, Edgar Degas: The Many Dimensions of a Master French Impressionist,
  The Dayton Art Institute, traveled to: Center for the Fine Arts, Miami, FL; Mississippi Museum of Art,
  Jackson, Mississippi; 1994, catalogue no. 81.

CATALOGUE RAISONNÉ:
Lemoisne 610; Russoli 758

Collection of The Dixon Gallery and Gardens, Gift of the Sara Lee Corporation, 1991.3

Jean Charles Cazin

(French, 1841-1901)

Landscape with Windmill

Oil on canvas
27 5/8 x 19 1/2 in.   70.4 x 49.6 cm.
Painted circa 1880

PROVENANCE:

Julia Wood Buckner, Memphis, Tennessee

The Dixon Gallery and Gardens, 1990

Collection of The Dixon Gallery and Gardens, Museum purchase - Margaret Hyde Fund, 1990.2

John Singer Sargent
(American, 1856-1925)

Ramón Subercaseaux in a Gondola

Oil on canvas mounted on panel
14 1/2 x 21 5/8 in.   36.8 x 55.0 cm.
Painted in 1880

PROVENANCE:
Mme. Ramón Subercaseaux, Santiago

Luis Subercaseaux, Santiago, Chile

M. Knoedler & Company, Inc., New York

Montgomery H. W. Ritchie, Clarendon, Texas, 1969

Cornelia Ritchie Bivins, Amarillo, Texas

The Dixon Gallery & Gardens, 1996

EXHIBITED:
Chicago, Sargent, Whistler, and Mary Cassatt, The Art Institute of Chicago
 and The Metropolitan Museum of Art, 1954, catalogue no. 44, p. 47,
 illustrated as Señor Subercaseaux in a Gondola in Venice, 1880.
New York, Americans in Venice, 1879-1913, Coe Kerr Gallery, 1983, catalogue no. 29.

SELECTED REFERENCES:
Charles Merrill Mount. John Singer Sargent, a Biography. New York, 1955, p. 428, catalogue no. 8017.
David McKibbin. "Check List of Sargent's Portraits," p. 125 in the catalogue of the
 exhibition Sargent's Boston, Museum of Fine Arts Boston, 1956.
Hugh Honour and John Flemming. The Venetian Hours of Henry James,
 Whistler and Sargent. Boston, p. 56.

CATALOGUE RAISONNÉ:
This work will be included in the forthcoming Sargent catalogue raisonné
being prepared by Richard Ormand for Adelson Galleries, Inc., New York.

Collection of The Dixon Gallery and Gardens,
Gift of Cornelia Ritchie Bivins, 1996.2.1

Stanislas-Victor-Édouard Lépine
(French, 1835-1892)

The Island of Grand Jatte in Summer

Signed lower right: S. Lépine
Oil on canvas
17 7/8 x 20 7/8 in.   45.4 x 52.7 cm.
Painted circa 1877-1882

PROVENANCE:
Joseph Reinach, Paris

Arthur Tooth and Sons, Ltd., London, 1968

Mr. and Mrs. Hugo Dixon, 1968

The Dixon Gallery and Gardens, 1975

EXHIBITED:
Paris, Lépine, Galerie Rosenberg, 1906, catalogue no. 36.

Huntington, New York, Illuminations: Images of Landscape in France, 1855-1885,
   Heckscher Museum, traveled to: The Walters Museum, Baltimore; The Dixon Gallery and Gardens, Memphis; 1990, catalogue no. 47.

CATALOGUE RAISONNÉ:
Schmit (1993) 404

Collection of The Dixon Gallery and Gardens,
Bequest of Mr. and Mrs. Hugo Dixon, 1975.21

Mary Cassatt
(American/French School, 1845-1926)

The Visitor

Oil and gouache on canvas
27 1/4 x 22 1/2 in.   69.2 x 57.2 cm.
Painted circa 1880

PROVENANCE:

Dikran G. Kélékian

Sale, Dikran Kélékian Collection, New York, January 31, 1922, no. 135

Private Collection, France

Durand-Ruel, Inc., New York

Private Collection, Paris

Sale, Maurice & Philippe Rheims, Vente par le ministre de Maurice Rheims
 et Philippe Rheims, Paris, November 29, 1962, no. 31

Howard Young, New York

Sale, Christie's, London, Impressionist and Modern Paintings, Drawings and Sculpture, March 27, 1973, lot no. 56

Private Collection, London

Sale, Palais des Congrès, Vente aux Enchrès Publiques Versailles, March 3, 1974, lot no. 76

Arthur Tooth & Sons, London

Mr. and Mrs. Hugo Dixon, 1974

The Dixon Gallery and Gardens, 1976

EXHIBITED:
New York, Mary Cassatt Exhibition,
  Wildenstein & Company, 1947, catalogue no. 6.
Paris, Collection Kélékian: Tableaux de L'Ecole Française Moderne,
  Place Vendome, 1920, catalogue no. 3.
San Jose, Mary Cassatt and Edgar Degas,
  San Jose Museum of Art, 1981, catalogue no. 29.

CATALOGUE RAISONNÉ:
Breeskin 83

Collection of The Dixon Gallery and Gardens, Bequest of Mr. and Mrs. Hugo Dixon, 1975.28

Claude Monet
(French 1840-1926)

Port of Dieppe, Evening

Inscribed with estate stamp lower right: Claude Monet (Lugt 1819b)
Oil on canvas
23 x 28 1/2 in.   58.5 x 72.4 cm.
Painted in 1882

PROVENANCE:
Michel Monet, Giverny

Leitner Collection, Paris

Marlborough Gallery, London

Montgomery H. W. Ritchie, Clarendon, Texas, 1963

The Dixon Gallery and Gardens, 1996

EXHIBITED:
Bâle, Impressionisten, Kunsthalle, 1949, no. 222.
New York, Claude Monet: Seasons and Moments,
  The Museum of Modern Art, 1960, catalogue no. 30, p. 61.
Dallas, Texas, Impressionist and Modern Masters in Dallas,
  Dallas Museum of Art, 1989, catalogue no. 66.

CATALOGUE RAISONNÉ:
Wildenstein (1979) 706. This work will be included
  in the forthcoming Monet catalogue raisonné being produced by Bea Rehders, Paris.

Collection of The Dixon Gallery and Gardens,
Gift of Montgomery H. W. Ritchie, 1996.2.7

Edmond Georges Grandjean
(French, 1844-1908)

A Coach Stop on the Place de Passy

Signed lower right: E. Grandjean
Oil on canvas
67 1/8 x 84 11/16 in.   172.4 x 215.0 cm.
Painted circa 1882

PROVENANCE:

Private Collection, England

Sale, Sotheby's, London, June 19, 1991, lot no. 192

The Dixon Gallery and Gardens, 1993

EXHIBITED:

Paris, Salon, 1882, catalogue no. 1223, p. 242.

Collection of The Dixon Gallery and Gardens,
Gift of The Bodine Company, 1993.1

Jean-Louis Forain
(French, 1852-1931)

Woman with a Fan

Signed lower right: J. L. Forain
Pastel on paper
35 x 31 in.   88.9 x 78.7 cm.
Executed circa 1883

PROVENANCE:

Durand Ruel, Paris, circa 1886

Mme. Lanvin, Paris

Galerie Brame et Lorenceau, Paris

Peter Findlay Gallery, New York

Hirschl and Adler Galleries, Inc., New York

Private Collection, Paris

The Dixon Gallery and Gardens, 1987

EXHIBITED:
Paris, 8me Exposition de Peinture, 1886, catalogue no. 33.
Washington, DC, The New Painting - Impressionism 1874-1886, National Gallery of Art,
   traveled to: San Francisco, The Fine Arts Museum of San Francisco,
   M. H. de Young Memorial Museum, 1986, catalogue no. 142, p. 455.
Amsterdam, Jean-Louis Forain: The Impressionist Years, Van Gogh Museum, traveled to:
   Glasgow, The Burrell Collection; Lausanne, Fondation de L'Hermitage; Paris, Galerie Hopkins-Thomas, 1995, catalogue no. 17.

Collection of The Dixon Gallery and Gardens, Museum Purchase,
partially supported by Mrs. James D. Robinson, Mrs. John Sneed Williams
and the estate of Louise Richardson Dodd, 1987.2

Edgar Degas
(French, 1834-1917)

Dancer Adjusting Her Shoe

Pastel on paper
19 x 24 in.   47.5 x 60.0 cm.
Executed in 1885

PROVENANCE:

Durand-Ruel, New York, circa 1946

M. Knoedler & Company, Inc., New York, 1959

Mr. and Mrs. Hugo Dixon, 1959

The Dixon Gallery and Gardens, 1976

EXHIBITED:
New York, Degas, Wildenstein and Company, 1960, catalogue no. 44.
New York, Edgar Degas, Acquavella Galleries, Inc., 1978, catalogue no. 33.
Tübingen, Germany, Edgar Degas: Pastelle, Ölskizzen, Zeichnungen, Kunsthalle Tübingen,
traveled to: National Gallery, Berlin, 1984, catalogue no. 164.
Washington, DC, Degas - The Dancers, National Gallery of Art, 1985, catalogue no. 40.

CATALOGUE RAISONNÉ:
Lemoisne 826; Russoli 818

SELECTED REFERENCES:
Robert Gordon and Andrew Forge, Degas,
  Harry N. Abrams, Inc., 1987, p. 277, illustrated p. 196.
Richard Thomson, Edgar Degas Waiting,
  Getty Museum Studies in Art, Malibu, California, 1995, p. 19.

Collection of The Dixon Gallery and Gardens, Bequest of Mr. and Mrs. Hugo Dixon, 1975.6

Eugène-Louis Boudin
(French, 1824-1898)

Beach Scene, Villerville

Signed lower right: E. Boudin
Oil on canvas
19 5/8 x 29 1/4 in.   49.8 x 74.3 cm.
Painted circa 1885

PROVENANCE:
Gerard Collection, Paris

Mr. V. B. Hill, London

Sale, Sotheby's, London, February 20, 1959, lot 92

Arthur Tooth & Sons, London

Montgomery H. W. Ritchie, Clarendon, Texas, 1959

The Dixon Gallery and Gardens, 1996

EXHIBITED:
London, Eugene Boudin 1824-1898, Marlborough Fine Art, Ltd., 1958, catalogue no. 65.

CATALOGUE RAISONNÉ:
Schmit (1973) 3218

Collection of The Dixon Gallery and Gardens, Gift of Montgomery H. W. Ritchie and Museum Purchase, 1996.2.19

Pierre-Auguste Renoir
(French, 1841-1919)

The Wave

Signed and dated lower left: Renoir 82
Oil on canvas
21 3/8 x 25 3/4 in.   54.3 x 65.4 cm.

PROVENANCE:

Van Diemen-Lilienfeld Galleries, New York

Montgomery H. W. Ritchie, Clarendon, Texas, 1949

Cornelia Ritchie Bivins, Amarillo, Texas

The Dixon Gallery and Gardens, 1996

EXHIBITED:
Dallas, Texas, Impressionist and Modern Masters in Dallas,
  Dallas Museum of Art, 1989, catalogue no. 90.

CATALOGUE RAISONNÉ:
This work will be included in the forthcoming supplement
  to the Renoir catalogue raisonné being produced by François Daulte.

Collection of The Dixon Gallery and Gardens, Gift of Cornelia Ritchie Bivins and Museum Purchase, 1996.2.12

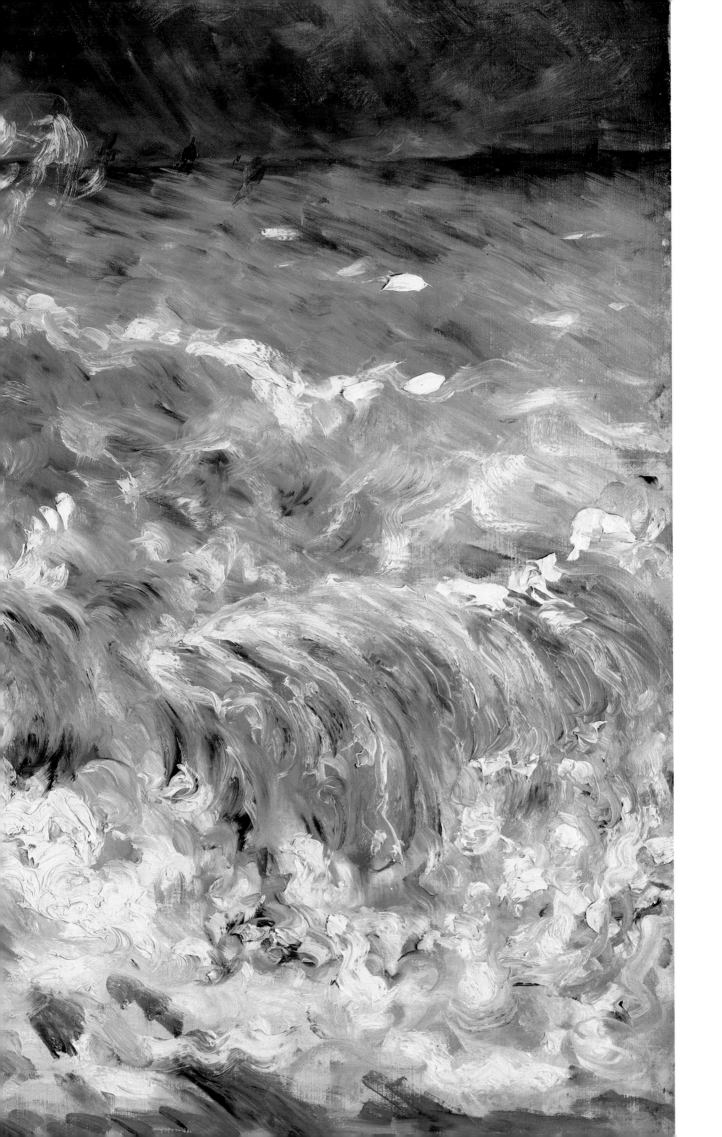

Georges Seurat
(French, 1859-1891)

The Picnic

Oil on panel
6 3/8 x 10 in.   16.2 x 25.4 cm.
Painted circa 1885

PROVENANCE:

Inventaire posthume, Atelier Seurat, May 3, 1891, no. 33, Leon Appert, Paris

Octave Mirbeau, Paris

Mme Vve Mirbeau, Paris

Sale, Galerie Durand-Ruel, Vente Octave Mirbeau, Paris, February 24, 1919, no. 50

Galerie Bernheim-Jeune, Paris

Percy Moore Turner

Galerie Bernheim-Jeune, Paris

R. A. Wilson, London

Mouradian et Van Leer

Félix Fénéon, Paris

Sale, Hotel Drouot, Collection Félix Fénéon, Paris, December 4, 1941

M. Fabiani Wildenstein & Company, New York

Montgomery H. W. Ritchie, Clarendon, Texas, 1957

The Dixon Gallery and Gardens, 1996

EXHIBITED:
Paris, Georges Seurat, Galerie Paul Rosenberg, 1936, catalogue no. 8.
London, Seurat and His Contemporaries,
  Galerie Wildenstein, 1937, catalogue no. 58.
Dallas, Texas, Impressionist and Modern Masters in Dallas,
  Dallas Museum of Art, 1989, catalogue no. 98.

SELECTED REFERENCES:
Inventaire posthume, Atelier Seurat, 1891.
Seurat, La Revue Blanche, Paris 1900, no. 20.
Julius Meier-Graefe. Entwickelungsgeschichte der Modernen Kunst:
  Vergleichende Betrachtung der Bildenden Künste, als Beitrag zu einer Neuen Aesthetik. Stuttgart: Verlag Jul Hoffmann, 1904, p. 232.
Gustave Coquiot. Seurat. Paris: Albin Michel, éditeur, 1924, p. 247. Jacques de Laprade. Georges Seurat. Monaco:
  Les Documents d'Art, 1945, p. 96, illustrated p. 30.
Henri Dorra and John Rewald. Seurat: L'Oeuvre Peint Biographie et Catalogue Critique.
  Paris: Les Beaux-Arts, 1959, no. 102, illustrated p. 109.

CATALOGUE RAISONNÉ:
De Hauke 143

Collection of The Dixon Gallery and Gardens, Gift of Montgomery H. W. Ritchie, 1996.2.14

Henri Stanislas Rouart
(French, 1833-1912)

Woman Playing the Guitar

Signed lower right: Henri Rouart
Oil on canvas
23 3/4 x 28 3/4 in.   60.5 x 72.9 cm.
Painted circa 1885-1890

PROVENANCE:

Hotel Drouot, Paris

Hammer Galleries, New York, 1971

Plaza Art Gallery, New York

Hammer Galleries, New York, 1977

The Dixon Gallery and Gardens, 1977

Collection of The Dixon Gallery and Gardens, Museum Purchase, 1977.5

Paul Signac
(French, 1863-1935)

St. Briac, the Cross of the Seamen

Signed lower right: P. Signac
Oil on canvas
12 1/2 x 17 3/4 in. 31.5 x 45.0 cm.
Painted in 1885

PROVENANCE:
Galerie Barbizon, Paris

René Long, Paris

Marlborough Fine Art Ltd., London

Mr. and Mrs. Hugo Dixon, 1964

The Dixon Gallery and Gardens, 1976

EXHIBITED:
London, Van Gogh's Life in his Drawings, Van Gogh's Relationship with Signac,
  Marlborough Fine Art, Ltd., 1962, catalogue no. 76.
Paris, Signac, Musée du Louvre, 1964, catalogue no. 12.
St. Petersburg, Florida, French Marine Painters of the Nineteenth Century,
  Museum of Fine Arts, 1985, catalogue no. 23.

SELECTED REFERENCES:
Sotheby's. Impressionist and Modern Paintings and Sculpture. London, July 2, 1969, lot 47.
Francoise Cachin. Paul Signac. Paris, 1971, p. 10, no. 6.

Collection of The Dixon Gallery and Gardens,
Bequest of Mr. and Mrs. Hugo Dixon, 1975.14

Paul Gauguin
(French, 1848-1903)

Bather in Front of the Port of Pont-Aven

Signed and dated lower left: P. Gauguin '86
Oil on canvas
31 1/2 x 23 1/8 in.   80.0 x 58.7 cm.

PROVENANCE:
Private Collection, Paris

Ambroise Vollard, Paris

Mme. de Galea, Paris

E. Van Wisselingh, Amsterdam

Mrs. Gustave Berne, Great Neck, Long Island

Sale, Parke-Bernet, New York, April 14, 1965, lot no. 52

The Lefevre Gallery, London, 1966

Mr. and Mrs. Hugo Dixon, 1966

The Dixon Gallery and Gardens, 1976

EXHIBITED:
Paris, Galerie Boussod Valladon, January 1888.
Paris, Gauguin, Durand-Ruel Galleries, 1891.
London, Leicester Gallery, 1912.
Paris, Galerie Bernheim-Jeune, 1921.
Paris, Paysage de France, Bernheim-Jeune Gallery, 1961.
Cincinnati, The Early Work of Paul Gauguin, The Cincinnati Art Museum, 1971.

SELECTED REFERENCES:
Félix Fénéon, Revue Independants, Calendrier, Paris, January 1888, p. 170.
F. M. Sugana, L'Opera Completa di Gauguin, Milan, 1972, no. 42.

CATALOGUE RAISONNÉ:
Wildenstein, (1964) 198. This work will be included in
  the forthcoming Gauguin catalogue raisonné being produced
  by Sylvie Crussard at Wildenstein Institute.

Collection of The Dixon Gallery and Gardens, Bequest of Mr. and Mrs. Hugo Dixon, 1975.30

Berthe Morisot
(French, 1841-1895)

Peasant Girl Among Tulips

Signed lower left: B. Morisot
Oil on canvas
25 3/4 x 28 11/16 in.   65.2 x 72.8 cm.
Painted in 1890

PROVENANCE:

Tadamara Hayashi, Paris, circa 1896

Theodore Duret, Paris

Paul Rosenberg Gallery, Paris, until 1926

A. Conger Goodyear, New York, 1926

Albright-Knox Gallery, Buffalo, 1966

Wildenstein and Co., New York, 1974

The Dixon Gallery and Gardens, 1981

EXHIBITED:
Paris, Berthe Morisot, Galeries Durand-Ruel, 1896, catalogue no. 43.
Paris, Exposition Berthe Morisot, Galerie Bernheim-Jeune, 1919, catalogue no. 60.
Buffalo, New York, A Selection of Paintings of the French Modern School
  from the Collection of A. C. Goodyear, Albright Art Gallery, 1928, catalogue no. 37.
San Francisco, French Paintings from the Fifteenth Century to the Present Day,
  California Palace of the Legion of Honor, 1934, catalogue no. 130.
Chicago, Berthe Morisot, The Arts Club, 1943, catalogue no. 27.
New York, Berthe Morisot, Wildenstein, 1960, catalogue no. 60.
Buffalo, New York, Paintings, Sculptures, Drawings, Prints
  Collected by A. Conger Goodyear, Albright-Knox Art Gallery, 1966, catalogue no. 27.

SELECTED REFERENCES:
L. Rouart. Berthe Morisot. Paris, 1941, p. 10.
E. Mongan. Berthe Morisot-Drawings, Pastels, Watercolor, Paintings. New York, 1960, p. 121.
Anne Higonnet. Berthe Morisot's Images of Women. Cambridge, 1992, p. 17-18.

CATALOGUE RAISONNÉ:
Bataille 257

Collection of The Dixon Gallery and Gardens,
Museum Purchase, 1981.1

Daniel Ridgway Knight
(American, 1839-1924)

The Newspaper

Signed lower left: Ridgway Knight, Paris
Watercolor on paper
21 x 14 in.   53.3 x 35.6 cm.
Executed circa 1890

PROVENANCE:

Knoedler Galleries, New York

Keny & Johnson Gallery, Columbus, Ohio

The Dixon Gallery and Gardens, 1990

CATALOGUE RAISONNÉ:
 This work will be included in the forthcoming Ridgway Knight
   catalogue raisonné being prepared by Howard Rehs, Rehs Galleries, New York.

The Dixon Gallery and Gardens, Museum Purchase - Martha R. Robinson Family Fund, 1990.7

Gaston De La Touche
(French, 1854-1913)

The Joyous Festival

Signed lower left: Gaston La Touche
Oil on canvas
82 3/8 x 114 1/2 in. 209.4 x 290.7 cm.
Painted circa 1890-1910

PROVENANCE:

Sale, Paris, February 27, 1909

Sale, Paris, December 4-5, 1918

Hirschl and Adler Gallery, New York

Sale, Sotheby Parke Bernet, Important 19th Century European Paintings,
  New York, May 28, 1981, no. 124

Private Collection, Florida

Sale, Sotheby's, New York, Important 19th Century European Paintings,
  Drawings, and Watercolors, October 28, 1986, no. 120

The Dixon Gallery and Gardens, 1986

Collection of The Dixon Gallery and Gardens, Gift of Mrs. James D. Robinson, 1986.3

Horatio Walker
(Canadian, 1856-1938)

Returning from the Fields
Signed and dated lower left: Horatio Walker, 1891
Pastel and gouache on paper
24 1/2 x 19 3/4 in.   62.2 x 50.1 cm.

PROVENANCE:
J. D. Cox, Cleveland, Ohio

Mrs. Lyle Bentzen (his daughter), Sheridon, Wyoming

The Dixon Gallery and Gardens, 1978

Collection of The Dixon Gallery and Gardens, Gift of Mrs. Lyle Bentzen, 1978.9

Eugène-Louis Boudin
(French, 1824-1898)

The Beach at Benerville, Low Tide

Signed and dated lower right: Benerville E. Boudin 92
Oil on canvas
19 1/8 x 28 5/8 in.   48.5 x 72.7 cm.

PROVENANCE:

Amedee Barincou, Bordeaux

Sale, Galeries George Petit, Catalogue des Tableaux Modernes...
  M. Barincou Collection, Paris, June 6, 1906, lot no. 12

Juan C. Labourdette, Buenos Aires

Arthur Tooth & Sons, Ltd., London, 1968

Mr. and Mrs. Hugo Dixon, 1968

The Dixon Gallery and Gardens, 1976

EXHIBITED:
London, Recent Acquisitions XXIII, Arthur Tooth & Sons, Ltd., 1968, catalogue no. 4.

SELECTED REFERENCES:
 G. Jean-Aubry. La Vie et l'oeuvre d'après les lettres et les documents
 inédits d'Eugène Boudin. Paris: La Bibliothèque des Arts, 1968, p. 167.

CATALOGUE RAISONNÉ:
Schmit (1973) 2944

Collection of The Dixon Gallery and Gardens,
 Bequest of Mr. and Mrs. Hugo Dixon, 1975.20

Maurice Prendergast
(American, 1859-1924)

Woman Drinking Tea

Signed lower left: Prendergast
Watercolor on paper
10 1/2 x 4 1/4 in.   26.7 x 10.8 cm.
Executed circa 1893-94

PROVENANCE:
Robert Stark

Freya Stark (his daughter)

Wildenstein & Company, New York

Montgomery H. W. Ritchie, Clarendon, Texas, 1963

The Dixon Gallery and Gardens, 1996

CATALOGUE RAISONNÉ:
Prendergast 582

Collection of The Dixon Gallery and Gardens, Gift of Montgomery H. W. Ritchie, 1996.2.11

Camille Pissarro
(French, 1830-1903)

View from the Artist's Studio at Éragny

Signed and dated lower left: C. Pissarro 94
Oil on panel
21 1/4 x 25 1/2 in.   54 x 64.7 cm.

PROVENANCE:
Private Collection, Paris

Arthur Tooth & Sons, London

Montgomery H. W. Ritchie, Clarendon, Texas, 1954

The Dixon Gallery and Gardens, 1996

EXHIBITED:
Pissarro, Sisley, Renoir, Guillaumin, Galerie Aktuaryus, 1938, catalogue no. 7.

CATALOGUE RAISONNÉ:
Venturi 868

Collection of The Dixon Gallery and Gardens, Gift of Montgomery H. W. Ritchie, 1996.2.9

Eugène-Louis Boudin
(French, 1824-1898)

Venice. Santa Maria Della Salute and the Custom-House.

Signed and dated lower left: Venise E. Boudin '95
Oil on panel
9 1/2 x 19 1/8 in.   24.1 x 48.5 cm.

PROVENANCE:

Sale, Hotel Drouot, Paris, June 20, 1947, lot no. 44

Galerie Charpentier, Paris

Marlborough Fine Arts, Ltd., London, 1957

Mr. and Mrs. Hugo Dixon, 1958

The Dixon Gallery and Gardens, 1976

EXHIBITED:

London, XIXth and XX Century European Masters, Marlborough Fine Art, Ltd., 1957,
   catalogue no. 6, illustrated p. 17 as Panorama de Venise, prise de S. Giorgio.

CATALOGUE RAISONNÉ:

Schmit (1973) 3387

Collection of The Dixon Gallery and Gardens, Bequest of Mr. and Mrs. Hugo Dixon, 1975.3

Pierre Bonnard
(French, 1867-1947)

Rue Tholozé

Signed lower left: Bonnard
Oil on cardboard
20 x 26 in.   50.8 x 66.0 cm.
Painted circa 1895

PROVENANCE:

J.W. Freshfield, Esquire, 1948

M.D. Oliphant

Arthur Tooth & Sons, Ltd., London

Montgomery H. W. Ritchie, Clarendon, Texas, 1955

The Dixon Gallery and Gardens, 1996

EXHIBITED:

London, Adams Gallery, June 1948.

Edinburgh, Exhibition of Paintings by Pierre Bonnard and Edouard Vuillard,
  Royal Scottish Academy, 1948, catalogue no. 6.

Dallas, Texas, Impressionist and Modern Masters in Dallas,
  Dallas Museum of Art, 1989, catalogue no. 5.

CATALOGUE RAISONNÉ:

Dauberville 155

Collection of The Dixon Gallery and Gardens,
  Gift of Montgomery H. W. Ritchie and Museum Purchase, 1996.2.2

Pierre-Auguste Renoir

(French, 1841-1919)

The Picture Book

Oil on canvas
15 1/2 x 12 1/2 in.   39.4 x 31.7 cm.
Painted circa 1895

PROVENANCE:

Sale, Hotel Drouot, Collection of Eugene Blot, Paris, May 10, 1906, no. 63, p. 30-31

Charles Harrison Tweed, New York

Mrs. B. Duval Chambers (his daughter), New York

Graham B. Blaine (her nephew), Boston

Hirschl and Adler Galleries, New York

The Dixon Gallery and Gardens, 1978

EXHIBITED:

Nagoya, Renoir Retrospective Exhibition, Nagoya City Art Museum, traveled to:
  Hiroshima Museum of Art, Hiroshima; Nara Prefectural Museum of Art, Nara, 1988-89, no. 49.
Balingen, Das Ewig Weiblich: L'Eternel Féminin von Renoir bis Picasso, Stadthalle Balingen, 1996, catalogue no. 6.

Collection of The Dixon Gallery and Gardens, Museum Purchase, 1978.4

Henri Matisse
(French, 1869-1954)

The Palace, Belle Isle

Signed lower right: Henri Matisse
Oil on canvas
12 3/4 x 15 3/4 in.   32.5 x 40.0 cm.
Painted circa 1896-97

PROVENANCE:

M. Bader, Strasbourg, France, circa 1931

Countess N. de Navarro, Monte Carlo and Glen Head

M. Knoedler and Company, New York

Schoneman Galleries, New York, 1965

Mr. and Mrs. Hugo Dixon, 1965

The Dixon Gallery and Gardens, 1976

EXHIBITED:
Basle, Belle Ile en Mer, Kunsthalle, 1931, no. 4.

Collection of The Dixon Gallery and Gardens, Bequest of Mr. and Mrs. Hugo Dixon, 1975.15

William Merritt Chase

(American, 1849-1916)

Portrait of a Lady

Signed and dated lower right: Chase 96
Oil on panel
14 5/8 x 10 1/2 in.   36.6 x 26.3 cm.

Berthe Noufflard
(French, 1886-1971)

Model Before a Chinese Screen

Signed and dated: Berthe 1908
Oil on canvas
18 1/8 x 15 in.   46.0 x 38.0 cm.

PROVENANCE:
Genevieve Noufflard and Henriette Guy-Loe

The Dixon Gallery and Gardens, 1990

EXHIBITED:
Memphis, Heirs to Impressionism: Andre and Berthe Noufflard,
  The Dixon Gallery and Gardens, traveled to: Meridian House International, Washington, DC;
  Oklahoma Museum of Art; Museum of Fine Arts, St. Petersburg, Florida;
  Philharmonic Performing Arts Center Galleries, Naples, Florida; Fort Wayne Art Museum, Fort Wayne, Indiana;
  French Embassy Gallery, New York, 1989-90, catalogue no. 5.

Collection of The Dixon Gallery and Gardens,
Gift of Henriette Noufflard Guy-Loe and Genevieve Noufflard, 1990.5

Theodore Earl Butler
(American, 1861-1937)

Grainstacks, Giverny

Oil on canvas
21 3/8 x 28 7/8 in.   54.4 x 73.2 cm.
Painted circa 1897

PROVENANCE:
Lili Butler and Roger Toulgouat

Jean-Marie Toulgouat (artist's grandson), France

Spanierman Gallery, New York

The Dixon Gallery and Gardens, 1991

EXHIBITED:
New York, Masters of American Art 1860-1950, Spanierman Gallery, 1991.

SELECTED REFERENCES:
Richard H. Love. Theodore Earl Butler: Emergence from Monet's Shadow.
  Chicago: Haase-Mumm Publishing Co., Inc., 1985.

CATALOGUE RAISONNÉ:
This work will be included in the forthcoming
  Butler catalogue raisonné being prepared by Patrick Bertrand.

Collection of The Dixon Gallery and Gardens, Museum Purchase by the Dixon Life Members Society, 1991.4

Maurice Prendergast
(American, 1859-1924)

Riva Degli Schiavone, Castello

Signed lower right: MB Prendergast
Watercolor on paper
14 1/8 x 10 5/8 in.   35.8 x 27.0 cm.
Executed in 1898

PROVENANCE:
Charles Prendergast, 1924

Mrs. Charles Prendergast, 1948

Robert Brady

Coe Kerr Gallery

Montgomery H. W. Ritchie, Clarendon, Texas, 1983

The Dixon Gallery and Gardens, 1996

EXHIBITED:
Art Institute of Chicago, 1900, no. 70.
Macbeth Gallery, 1900, no. 3, as Riva degli Schiavoni, Venice.
Detroit, 1901, no. 17, as River degli Schiavoni.
Art Institute of Chicago, 1905, no. 361, as The Riva, Venice.
New York, Americans in Venice, 1879-1913, Coe Kerr Gallery, 1983,
  catalogue no. 63, as Riva degli Schiavoni, Castello.

CATALOGUE RAISONNÉ:
Prendergast 704

Collection of The Dixon Gallery and Gardens, Gift of Montgomery H. W. Ritchie and Museum Purchase, 1996.2.10

Maximilien Luce
(French, 1858-1941)

The Cathedral at Gisors, View of the Ramparts

Signed and dated lower right: Luce '98
Oil on canvas
27 7/8 x 35 1/2 in.   70.7 x 90.2 cm.

PROVENANCE:

H.V. Gort

Walter Feilchenfeld, Zurich

Collection Basmadjieff, Los Angeles

Sale, Sotheby's, July 3, 1968, lot no. 58

Sale, Christie's, London, November 28, 1972, lot no. 68

Arthur Tooth and Sons, Ltd., London, 1972

Mr. and Mrs. Hugo Dixon, 1972

The Dixon Gallery and Gardens, 1976

EXHIBITED:
Paris, Salon des Independents, Galerie Durand-Ruel, 1899, no. 104.
London, The Rim of Impressionism, Arthur Tooth & Sons, Ltd., 1965, no. 11.

SELECTED REFERENCES:
Richard Shone. The Post Impressionists. London, 1979, p. 49.
Philippe Cazeau. Maximilien Luce. Paris: Bibliotheque des Arts, 1982, p. 110.

CATALOGUE RAISONNÉ:
Bouin-Luce 516

Collection of The Dixon Gallery and Gardens, Bequest of Mr. and Mrs. Hugo Dixon, 1975.23

Kenyon Cox
(American, 1856-1919)

Hope and Memory

Signed and dated: Copyright 1900 by Kenyon Cox
Oil on canvas
42 x 26 1/4 in.   106.5 x 66.6 cm.

PROVENANCE:
Mr. J. D. Cox (artist's brother), Cleveland, Ohio

Mrs. Lyle Bentzen (his daughter), Sheridon, Wyoming

The Dixon Gallery and Gardens, 1978

EXHIBITED:
Maine, Americans and Paris, Colby College Museum of Art, 1990.

SELECTED REFERENCES:
H. W. Morgan. Kenyon Cox 1856-1919: A Life in American Art.
  Kent State University Press, 1992.

Collection of The Dixon Gallery and Garden, Gift of Mrs. Lyle Bentzen, 1978.10

Camille Pissarro
(French, 1830-1903)

The Jetty at Le Havre, High Tide, Morning Sun

Signed and dated lower right: C. Pissarro 1903
Oil on canvas
21 1/2 x 25 5/8 in.   54.7 x 65.2 cm.

PROVENANCE:

Lucien Pissarro

John Quinn

Sale, Gabriel Picard Auction House, John Quinn Collection,
  Paris, Oct. 28, 1926, lot no. 63

Hirschl and Adler Galleries

The Dixon Gallery and Gardens, 1979

EXHIBITED:
New York, Pissarro Exhibition, Durand-Ruel Galleries, 1936, catalogue no. 5.
New York, The Art of Camille Pissarro in Retrospect, Durand-Ruel Galleries, 1941, catalogue no. 2.
Tokyo, Retrospective, Camille Pissarro, Isetan Museum of Art,
  traveled to: Fukuoka Municipal Museum of Art, Fukuoka;
  Kyoto Municipal Museum of Art, Kyoto; 1984, catalogue no. 61.
Dallas, Texas, The Impressionist and the City: Pissarro's Series, Dallas Museum of Art,
  traveled to: Philadelphia Museum of Art, Philadelphia, Pennsylvania; Royal Academy of Arts, London; 1992-93.

CATALOGUE RAISONNÉ:
Venturi 1298

Collection of The Dixon Gallery and Gardens, Museum Purchase, 1979.5

Paul Cézanne
(French, 1839-1906)

Trees and Rocks Near The Château Noir

Oil on canvas
24 3/8 x 20 1/4 in.   62 x 51.5 cm.
Painted circa 1900-1906

PROVENANCE:

Ambroise Vollard, Paris (until 1936)

H. S. Southam, Ottawa

French Art Galleries, New York

M. Knoedler & Company, Inc., New York, 1944

Montgomery H. W. Ritchie, Clarendon, Texas, 1950

Cornelia Ritchie Bivins, Amarillo, Texas

The Dixon Gallery and Gardens, 1996

EXHIBITED:
New York, Cezanne, The Bignou Gallery, 1936,
  catalogue no. 29, illustrated as Environs de Tholouet.
London, The Cezanne Exhibition, Reid & Lefevre Gallery,
  1937, catalogue no. 26.
Palm Beach, The Post Impressionists and Their Followers,
  Society of the Four Arts, 1949, catalogue no. 33.
Dallas, Texas, Impressionist and Modern Masters in Dallas,
  Dallas Museum of Art, 1989, catalogue no. 21.

CATALOGUE RAISONNÉ:
Venturi 792, Orienti 722

Collection of The Dixon Gallery and Gardens, Gift of Cornelia Ritchie Bivins and Museum Purchase, 1996.2.20

Edouard Vuillard
(French, 1868-1940)

Still Life

Inscribed with estate stamp lower right: E. Vuillard (Lugt)
Tempera on paper mounted on panel
12 x 7 7/8 in.   30.3 x 20.0 cm.
Painted in 1905

PROVENANCE:

Hallsborough, London

Sale, Sotheby's, London, April 24, 1963, lot 83

Arthur Tooth & Sons, London

Montgomery H. W. Ritchie, Clarendon, Texas, 1963

The Dixon Gallery and Gardens, 1996

CATALOGUE RAISONNÉ:
This work will be included in the forthcoming
  Vuillard catalogue raisonné being prepared by Antoine Salomon.

Collection of The Dixon Gallery and Gardens, Gift of Montgomery H. W. Ritchie and Museum Purchase, 1996.2.18

Henri-Edmond Cross
(French, 1856-1910)

The Little Maure Mountains

Signed and dated lower right: Henri-Edmond Cross '09
Oil on canvas
12 1/4 x 21 in.   31 x 53.2 cm.

PROVENANCE:
M. Meyer, Zurich

Marlborough Fine Arts Ltd., London, circa 1960

Mr. and Mrs. Hugo Dixon, 1966

The Dixon Gallery and Gardens, 1976

EXHIBITED:
Paris, Exposition Henri-Edmond Cross, Bernheim Jeune & Company, 1910,
    catalogue no. 40. London, Masters of Modern Art from 1840-1960,
    Marlborough Fine Art, Ltd., 1960, catalogue no. 20.

Collection of The Dixon Gallery and Gardens, Bequest of Mr. and Mrs. Hugo Dixon, 1975.17

Romain Jarosz
(French, 1889-1932)

Village View

Signed lower left: R. Jarosz
Oil on canvas
25 1/2 x 31 7/8 in.   65.0 x 81 cm.

Allen Tucker
(American, 1866-1939)

Corn Shocks

Signed and dated lower right: A. Tucker, 1910
Oil on canvas
35 x 30 in.   88.9 x 76.2 cm.

PROVENANCE:

Allen Tucker Memorial Foundation, New York

The Dixon Gallery and Gardens, 1976

Collection of The Dixon Gallery and Gardens,
Gift of the Allen Tucker Memorial Foundation, 1976.2

Francis Tattegrain
(French, 1852-1915)

City Street

Signed lower left: Tattegrain
Oil on wood panel
11 1/8 x 9 1/8 in.   28.2 x 23.0 cm.

PROVENANCE:

Julia Wood Buckner, Memphis, Tennessee

The Dixon Gallery and Gardens, 1990

Collection of The Dixon Gallery and Gardens,
Museum purchase - Margaret Hyde Fund, 1990.3

Max Silbert

(Russian-French, b. 1871)

Lacemakers at Prayer in Ghent

Signed and dated lower right: Silbert 1914
Oil on canvas
47 1/4 x 57 1/2 in.   120.0 x 146.0 cm.

PROVENANCE:

Sale, Sotheby's, 19th Century European Paintings, Drawings, and Sculpture,
  February 24, 1988, lot 123

Pat Tigrett and Kerr Tigrett, Memphis, Tennessee

The Dixon Gallery and Gardens, 1991

Collection of The Dixon Gallery and Gardens, Gift of Pat Tigrett and her son, Kerr, 1991.2

Maurice Utrillo
(French, 1883-1955)

The Road to Puteaux

Signed lower right: Maurice Utrillo. V.
Oil on canvas
23 x 31 3/4 in.   58.4 x 80.6 cm.
Painted circa 1915

PROVENANCE:
Paul Guillaume, Paris

Madame Jean Walter (his widow), Paris

Margaret Thompson Biddle

Private Collection, Paris

Wildenstein & Company, New York

Montgomery H. W. Ritchie, Clarendon, Texas, 1963

Cornelia Ritchie Bivins, Amarillo, Texas

The Dixon Gallery and Gardens, 1996

EXHIBITED:
Pittsburgh, Pennsylvania, Maurice Utrillo, Pittsburgh Museum of Art,
  Carnegie Institute, 1963, catalogue no. 75.
Dallas, Texas, Impressionist and Modern Masters in Dallas,
  Dallas Museum of Art, 1989, catalogue no. 107.

CATALOGUE RAISONNÉ:
Pétridès 472

Collection of The Dixon Gallery and Gardens, Gift of Cornelia Ritchie Bivins, 1996.2.17

Pierre Bonnard
(French, 1867-1947)

Woman Picking Flowers

Signed lower left: Bonnard
Oil on panel
14 5/8 x 17 3/4 in.   37.2 x 45.1 cm.
Painted circa 1915

PROVENANCE:

Louis Besnard

Bernheim-Jeune Galerie, 1916

Art Moderne Galerie, Lucerne

Sir Cyril Radcliffe

David Tomlinson, England

Wildenstein & Company, Inc., New York, 1963

Mr. and Mrs. Hugo Dixon, 1963

The Dixon Gallery and Gardens, 1976

EXHIBITED:
London, Bonnard and His French Contemporaries, Lefevre Galleries, 1947,
  catalogue no. 14, illustrated as Femme Ramassant des Fleurs, circa 1920.
Edinburgh, Exhibition of Paintings by Pierre Bonnard & Edouard Vuillard,
  Royal Scottish Academy, 1948, catalogue no. 21, illustrated as Landscape with Woman Picking Flowers, circa 1915.
Zurich, Pierre Bonnard 1867-1947, Kunsthaus, 1949, catalogue no. 43,
  illustrated as Paysage avec femme cueillant des fleurs.
Tokyo, Pierre Bonnard, Isetan Museum of Art, traveled to:
  Nara Sogo Museum of Art, Sogo Museum of Art, Fukuoka Art Museum, 1991.

SELECTED REFERENCES:
Gustave Coquoit. Pierre Bonnard. Paris:
  Les editions Bernheim Jeune, 1922, n.p., illustrated.
Claude Roger-Marx. Pierre Bonnard. Paris:
  Librairie Gaillimard, 1924, p. 29.

CATALOGUE RAISONNÉ:
Dauberville 855

Collection of The Dixon Gallery and Gardens, Bequest of Mr. and Mrs. Hugo Dixon, 1975.9

Louis Aston Knight
(American, 1873-1948)

Reflecting Pool at Beaumont-le-Roger
Signed and inscribed lower left: Aston Knight, Paris
Oil on canvas
32 x 25 7/8 in.　　　81.3 x 65.7 cm.
Painted circa 1920-24

PROVENANCE:

Mr. and Mrs. George Knight

The Dixon Gallery and Gardens, 1990

SELECTED REFERENCES:
Herbert F. Johnson Museum of Art. A Pastoral Legacy: Paintings and Drawings
  by the American Artists Ridgway Knight and Aston Knight. Cornell University, Ithaca, NY, 1989.

Collection of The Dixon Gallery and Gardens, Gift of Mr. and Mrs. George Knight, 1990.12

Chaim Soutine
(Lithuanian/French School, 1894-1943)

Landscape at Cagnes

Signed lower left: Soutine
Oil on canvas
18 1/4 x 21 7/8 in.   46.3 x 55.5 cm.
Painted circa 1922

PROVENANCE:

Arthur Tooth & Sons, London

Montgomery H. W. Ritchie, Clarendon, Texas, 1957

The Dixon Gallery and Gardens, 1996

CATALOGUE RAISONNÉ:
This work will be included in the forthcoming supplement
  to the Soutine catalogue raisonné being prepared by Tuchman, Dunow, and Perls.

Collection of The Dixon Gallery and Gardens, Gift of Montgomery H. W. Ritchie, 1996.2.16

Georges Braque
(French, 1882-1963)

Pot of Anemones

Signed and dated lower left: G Braque 25
Oil on panel
22 1/8 x 21 5/8 in.   56.2 x 54.9 cm.

PROVENANCE:

John Sweeney, New York

Sam Jaffe, Beverly Hills

M. Knoedler & Company, Inc., New York

Montgomery H. W. Ritchie, Clarendon, Texas, 1953

Cornelia Ritchie Bivins, Amarillo, Texas

The Dixon Gallery and Gardens, 1996

EXHIBITED:
Dallas, Texas, Impressionist and Modern Masters in Dallas,
    Dallas Museum of Art, 1989, catalogue no. 14.

CATALOGUE RAISONNÉ:
Maeght 68

Collection of The Dixon Gallery and Gardens, Gift of Cornelia Ritchie Bivins and Museum Purchase, 1996.2.1

Raoul Dufy
(French, 1877-1953)

View Through a Window, Nice

Signed lower right: Raoul Dufy
Oil on canvas
35 1/2 x 28 1/4 in.   90.1 x 71.7 cm.
Painted circa 1925

PROVENANCE:

Dalzell Hatfield Gallery, Los Angeles

Montgomery H. W. Ritchie, Clarendon, Texas, 1950

Cornelia Ritchie Bivins, Amarillo, Texas

The Dixon Gallery and Gardens, 1996

EXHIBITED:
San Antonio, Texas, Raoul Dufy, Marion Koogler McNay Art Institute, 1980,
  catalogue no. 38, illustrated as Still Life Before a Window.
Dallas, Texas, Impressionist and Modern Masters in Dallas,
  Dallas Museum of Art, 1989, catalogue no. 33.

CATALOGUE RAISONNÉ:
Laffaille 1228

Collection of The Dixon Gallery and Gardens, Gift of Cornelia Ritchie Bivins and Museum Purchase, 1996.2.4

Marc Chagall
(Russian/French School, 1887-1985)

Bouquet of Flowers with Lovers

Signed lower right: Marc Chagall
Oil on canvas
17 3/4 x 12 3/4 in.   44.8 x 32.5 cm.
Painted in 1927

PROVENANCE:

J. K. Thannhauser, Berlin and New York

O. Spaeth

Arthur Tooth & Sons, Ltd., London, 1963

Sale, Sotheby's, London, April 24, 1963, p. 28, illustrated p. 44

Mr. and Mrs. Hugo Dixon, 1963

The Dixon Gallery and Gardens, 1976

EXHIBITED:

Utica, NY, Spaeth Collection: Paintings, Sculpture, Munson-Williams-Proctor Institute,
  1952, catalogue no. 6, illustrated as Still Life.
Princeton, NJ, The Spaeth Collection, Princeton University Art Gallery, November 1952.
Columbus, The Spaeth Collection, Columbus Gallery of Fine Arts,
  1955, catalogue no. 8, illustrated as Still Life.

Collection of The Dixon Gallery and Gardens, Bequest of Mr. and Mrs. Hugo Dixon, 1975.10

Marc Chagall

(Russian/French School, 1887-1985)

Dreamer

Signed and dated lower right: Marc Chagall 1945
Oil on canvas
28 1/2 x 21 1/2 in   72.3 x 54.6 cm

PROVENANCE:

James Johnson, New York, 1957

M. Knoedler & Company, Inc., New York, 1958

Montgomery H. W. Ritchie, Clarendon, Texas, 1960

Cornelia Ritchie Bivins, Amarillo, Texas

The Dixon Gallery and Gardens, 1996

SELECTED REFERENCES:
Isaac Kloomok. Marc Chagall: His Life and Work. New York, 1951, p. 92.

Collection of The Dixon Gallery and Gardens, Gift of Cornelia Ritchie Bivins, 1996.2.3

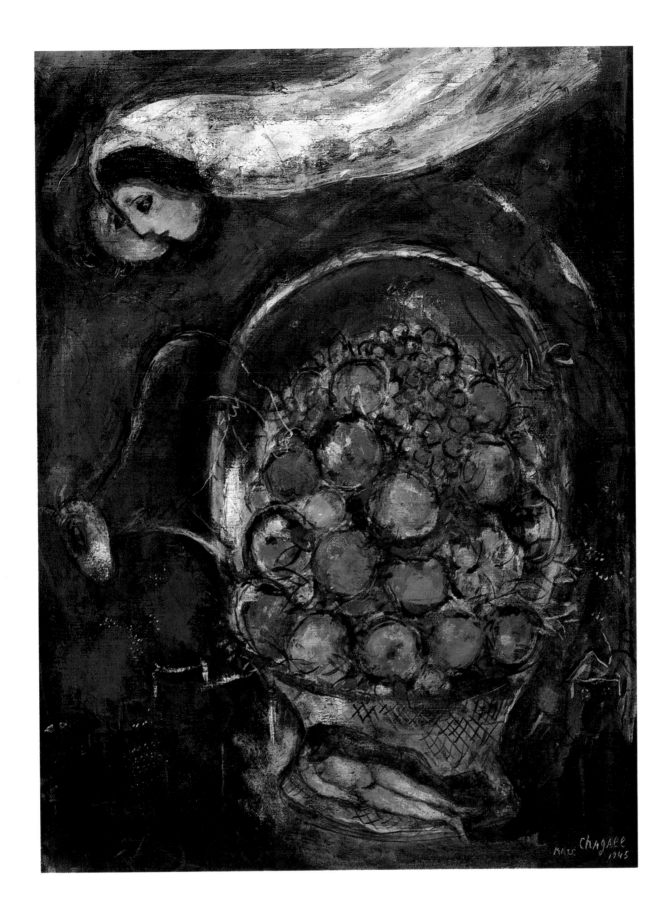

Pierre-Albert Marquet
(French, 1875-1947)

The Point of the Ile st. Louis

Signed lower right: Marquet
Oil on canvas
23 1/8 x 28 1/4 in.   58.7 x 71.8 cm.
Painted in 1928

PROVENANCE:

Madame Marcelle Martinet Marquet, Paris

Private Collection, Paris

Arthur Tooth and Sons, Ltd., London

Mr. and Mrs. Hugo Dixon, 1968

The Dixon Gallery and Gardens, 1976

EXHIBITED:
London, Paris-Londres, Arthur Tooth & Sons, Ltd., 1967.

CATALOGUE RAISONNÉ:
This work will be included in the forthcoming Marquet
  catalogue raisonné being prepared by Wildenstein Institute.

Collection of The Dixon Gallery and Gardens, Bequest of Mr. and Mrs. Hugo Dixon, 1975.19

Pierre-Albert Marquet
(French, 1875-1947)

Blue Boat at Porquerolles

Signed lower right: Marquet
Oil on canvas
17 1/2 x 23 1/4 in.   44.4 x 59.1 cm.
Painted in 1938

PROVENANCE:

Madame Marcelle Martinet Marquet, Paris

Montgomery H. W. Ritchie, Clarendon, Texas

The Dixon Gallery and Gardens, 1996

EXHIBITED:
Paris, Exposition de peintures et sculptures contemporaines,
  Palais des Papes, 1947, catalogue no. 111, as Porquerolles, 1939.
Paris, Marquet Exposition, Musée de Lyon, 1962,
  catalogue no. 72, as Bateau bleu à Porquerolles, 1938.
New York, Marquet, Knoedler Gallery, May 1964,
  catalogue no. 47, as Blue Boat at Porquerolles, 1939.

CATALOGUE RAISONNÉ:
This work will be included in the forthcoming Marquet
  catalogue raisonné being prepared by Wildenstein Institute.

Collection of The Dixon Gallery and Gardens, Gift of Montgomery H. W. Ritchie and Museum Purchase, 1996.2.5

Henry Moore
(English, 1898-1986)

Reclining Figure

Bronze with brown patina
length 6 1/4 in.   17.8 cm

Executed in 1945
Cast in an edition of nine, this figure was a working model
for a larger reclining figure, executed in 1945,
which was cast in an edition of seven.

PROVENANCE:

Sale, Christie's, London, June 12, 1970, lot 201

Mayor Gallery, London

Montgomery H. W. Ritchie, Clarendon, Texas, 1970

The Dixon Gallery and Gardens, 1995

SELECTED REFERENCES:
James Johnson Sweeney. Henry Moore. New York, 1946, p. 83 (illus. of another cast).
Will Gorhmann. The Art of Henry Moore. 1960, no. 36 (illus. of the terracotta).
David Sylvester, ed. Henry Moore, Sculpture and Drawings,
   1921-1948. Vol. I, New York, 1968, p. 16, no. 250.

CATALOGUE RAISONNÉ:
Lund Humphries 250

Collection of The Dixon Gallery and Gardens, Gift of Montgomery H. W. Ritchie, 1996.2.8

Photograph by André Kertész, 1952.

Index of Artists

Chronological Index

Index of Accession

The Dixon Gallery and Gardens

Donor to the Publication - Union Planters Bank, Memphis, Tennessee.
Color Photography by Pete Ceren Photography, Memphis, Tennessee.
Typographical composition in Eras by Scott Brooks, Memphis, Tennessee.

All text and illustrations were printed in offset lithography
using 150-line screen color separations on Karma 100 lb. text.
Cover was foil stamped on Strathmore Grandee Bordeaux Purple, 80 lb. cover.
Printing and color separations by Pinnacle Press, Memphis, Tennessee,

The book was designed by Elvis Kee, Memphis, Tennessee.

2500 perfect bound copies and 500 casebound copies of this book
have been published by The Dixon Gallery and Gardens, December 1996.